DIGITAL DISCIPLE

ADAM THOMAS

DIGITAL DISCIPLE

REAL CHRISTIANITY IN A VIRTUAL WORLD

Abingdon Press
Nashville

DIGITAL DISCIPLE
REAL CHRISTIANITY IN A VIRTUAL WORLD

Copyright © 2011 by Adam Thomas

All rights reserved.

This book is printed on acid-free paper.

Library of Congress Cataloging-in-Publication Data

Thomas, Adam.
    Digital disciple : real Christianity in a virtual world / Adam Thomas.
        p.   cm.
    ISBN 978-1-4267-1220-3 (pbk. : alk. paper)
    1. Christian life—Anglican authors.   2. Internet—Religious aspects—Christianity.
I. Title.
    BV4509.5.T484 2011
    248.4'8309051—dc22

                                                                            2011004393

Scripture quotations are from the Common English Bible. Copyright © 2011 by the Common English Bible. All rights reserved. Used by permission. (www.CommonEnglishBible.com)

11 12 13 14 15 16 17 18 19 20—10 9 8 7 6 5 4 3 2 1

MANUFACTURED IN THE UNITED STATES OF AMERICA

For
L. E. J.,
who between the writing
and the publishing
of this book became
(thanks be to God!)
L. E. T.

Contents

VIRTUAL PEOPLE

We call it an Internet "connection." On any given day, I know that an acquaintance from high school just had a baby shower. I know that an old college friend chose the strappy sandals. I know who had one too many at a party last night. Through my keyboard, LED monitor, wireless router, and ISP, I'm connected to several layers of people—my close friends, my acquaintances, strangers with similar interests, and the hordes of people with spelling so dreadful it would make Noah Webster weep.

But we could just as easily call it an Internet "isolation." While millions of little connections happen every day—from friends and relatives to subcultures and fan bases—these connections always happen remotely. I can see and hear people thousands of miles away using the warm box on my lap. But I can't touch using Facebook.† I can't taste a friend's tweets. And I sure can't smell

---

† *Facebook* (n.) The social network that I joined right after college because my then girlfriend wanted to say we were a couple on her pro-file. Ironically, this is also how I found out about her next boyfriend. (v.) To look someone up on the site or to use the site to send something to someone (e.g., "I Facebooked you last night and noticed that you like Taylor Swift too! I'll Facebook you the dates of her next tour!").

a Wikipedia entry. My senses are reduced by 60 percent. I have a contacts list on my Gmail account, but I rarely make *contact*. A wall of technology isolates me from you, and the more we use the Tech,[†] the more comfortable we feel hiding behind it. We develop a dependence on what can only be described oxymoronically as remote intimacy.

Yes, we are connected, but more often than not we connect remotely. Yes, I may know your favorite bands and books, but I may never know the timbre of your voice or how heavy your footfalls are. Yes, community forms on the Internet, but how can you share a meal or look someone in the eye via an online forum?

I make the observations found in this book from a vantage point overlooking a pair of intersections. The first intersection occurs where the opposing forces of connection and isolation meet. These two forces have been around since the Garden of Eden, but never have they been as coupled as the Internet makes them. The second intersection occurs at the junction between Tech culture and the greater reality of following Jesus Christ our Lord.

Following Jesus Christ is first and foremost about connection, about the arms of love reaching from the cross to embrace everyone. The Word became flesh in Jesus Christ in order that we

---

[†] I'll use the word *Tech* as an umbrella term for the Internet and the host of other technological advances of the last fifty years or so. The term entered my vocabulary via Fox's short-lived TV program *Dollhouse*, in which technology advances quickly and dangerously, to the point that people's personalities, memories, and essential humanity can be stripped from their bodies. (As a side note, those of us still lamenting the loss of *Firefly* wonder how Joss Whedon could ever agree to work with Fox again.)

might see more clearly the connection that God yearns for us to have with one another and with God. The Internet offers wonderful opportunities for connection, but they always come attached with the danger of isolation. Like most things in this life, we can't separate the danger from the opportunity; we can only hope to trend toward the opportunity while trying not to ignore the nature of the danger.

As the Internet continues to change the way we communicate and connect with one another, the opportunities and dangers grow increasingly intertwined. The trouble is that the speed of innovation has kept us from pausing, breathing deeply, and taking a hard look at technology's effects on our lives. Consider that a hundred years ago, people dashed and dotted with the telegraph and wrote long correspondences in perfect cursive. Seventy-five years ago, they shared a phone line with half a dozen neighbors and sat in front of the radio in the evening. Fifty years ago, they had their own telephone numbers and televisions. Twenty-five years ago, mobile phones and personal computers had begun the big, boxy stage of their evolutions. Fifteen years ago, my computer spent an agonizing forty-five seconds doing a fuzzy R2-D2 impression while attempting to dial up a connection to the Internet. Ten years ago, my family got our hands on a shiny new piece of technology called a cable modem, and the connection tripled in speed. Today, broadband allows connections of ease and immediacy. The breadth and depth of content online have now matched the blazing download rate; indeed (and I'm saying this with only the slightest hyperbole), I could live my whole life virtually and never notice the lack of fresh air and exercise.

3

We communicate more quickly, more frequently, more globally (and often more anonymously) than ever before. The Internet, once a harebrained idea hatched in a military think tank, has pervaded our lives and our society. Removing it would be like amputating not an arm or a leg, but a central nervous system. I know I'm not alone when I confess that, while I don't live my whole life virtually, I do almost everything online: shop, check baseball scores, read the news, watch TV, play games, chat with friends, research my sermons. I even met my wife through some combination of divine intervention and the Series of Tubes.†

As I view the intersections between connection and isolation, Tech culture and following Jesus, you should know that I make my observations from the perspective of a member of the first generation that has never known a world without the Internet. I'm a Millennial, one of the vanguard of the generation whose first members were born in 1982.‡ As one of the eldest of the Millennials, I remember artifacts such as Prodigy and CompuServe, which lost the evolutionary battle to AOL. I remember when Napster was new and innovative and not at all threatening to the music industry. I remember when *e-mail* caught the attention of spellcheck.

But I don't remember a time before *http* and *www* were more than just letters. I don't remember my father owning a computer

---

† "Series of Tubes" is late Senator Ted Stevens's famously inept description of the Internet, which has taken on the status of cult nickname.
‡ As Maxwell Smart would say, "Missed it by that much": I was born less than two weeks into 1983.

without a port for a phone cord. Ask younger members of the generation, and they won't even realize that computers came with phone ports rather than Ethernet ones. My first cell phone was for emergencies only because it had a paltry fifteen minutes a month. (Don't tell my dad, but most of my emergencies were of the pizza-ordering variety.) Younger Millennials have had cell phones since they were in elementary school. But from the eldest of us who remember the cretaceous period of dial-up to the youngest who were born with Bluetooth implants, we Millennials are dependent on the Tech, on all the gadgets and machines and Series of Tubes that connect us one to another and each to the world.

Of course, Millennials aren't the only ones affected by the rise of the Internet and associated Tech. GenXers, Boomers, and computer-savvy older people like my grandmother feel the strong current of the Internet pulling them online just as much. As a Millennial, I have felt this current pulling me since I could reach the keyboard. As a follower of Christ, I feel God moving in both my virtual and my real lives. Knowing that these dual influences are neither mutually exclusive nor entirely compatible gives rise to a series of questions.

How do the Tech's simultaneous forces of connection and isolation affect our walks with Christ? How does living in a virtual world influence living in both the physical and the spiritual ones? How do we maintain the body of Christ when the physical bodies we see and touch in church expand to include the virtual bodies we inhabit online? What place does prayer have in our instantaneous, Tech-driven world? Where do we keep our knowledge of

God when our preferred method of storing information has shifted to the external? How do we resist isolation while remaining plugged into the Series of Tubes? Now, I can speak only from my own experience. But I know that we humans are ineffective at arriving at the truth on our own, so I hope and pray that you will interact with my experience to delve more deeply into the truth revealed in Jesus Christ. Each of us has a call from God, each a ministry. Within each of the questions above, we find this fundamental one: How do we continue in the tradition of the personal nature of the ministry of Jesus in lives that are increasingly siphoned off into remote, disembodied, virtual space? I invite you to explore this question with me.

But first, you might be wondering why you should take what I say seriously. Who am I to write this book? Well, I claim neither special revelation from the Almighty nor a mandate from my generation. I'm just another disciple of Jesus Christ who has a few words to share with you. I endeavor to follow Christ wherever he leads me, but increasingly I find myself walking along the data streams and fiber-optic paths of the virtual world. Is it possible that Jesus might find me and I might find him on those virtual paths? Is it possible that God can use the Tech to create better followers of Jesus Christ? I am convinced that the answer is a resounding *yes*, but a yes stamped with a necessary warning label. Our Tech-driven world is changing rapidly, and we are changing with it. Unlike the great cloud of Christian witnesses that has preceded us, we're not simply earthbound, pavement-pounding disciples of Jesus Christ. The Tech has added a new dimension to our lives; we are physical, emotional, spiritual, and now *virtual* people. But I believe that God continues to move through every facet of our existence, and that makes us new kinds of followers. We are digital disciples.

DESERTED ISLANDS

The new dimension of virtuality that the Tech has added to our lives has brought with it new locations, new situations, and yes, new opportunities and dangers. We are pioneers moving not along a riverbank in rickety covered wagons but along the virtual paths marked by cell towers and wi-fi hot spots.[†] The lay of the land has changed, so to speak, and our new virtual environments are affecting us on multiple levels, which we will address over the course of this book. But before entering fully into our discussion of connection and isolation, we must address briefly the influence that the new frontier of the Tech has on our identity as social creatures.

To explore this influence, join me in a quick illustration. You attend a party; say, a company Christmas party. Spouses and children have been invited, so there's a mix of generations milling about the lobby. On the buffet table sit cheese and crackers and

---

[†] Given the fact that the Tech has generated another new frontier, it's no surprise that one of the first popular computer games was *Oregon Trail*, a game that attempted to educate students about the pioneering days of the nineteenth century by simulating a trip to the West Coast in a covered wagon. Nearly forty years since its creation, the game continues to draw players today. More often than not, the game ends, as it has for so many players over the years, with these fateful words: "You have died of dysentery."

7

one rather forlorn-looking vegetable tray. The eggnog comes in two varieties, one for grown-ups only. Bing Crosby croons softly over the PA system. Adults chat in that awkward way that always happens when home and work collide. One man's laugh keeps rising over the low murmur in the room. Everyone attempts to avoid the mistletoe because that one creepy guy from the mailroom has claimed the territory underneath it.

Walking back from disposing of your paper plate and plastic cup, you notice a trio of people sitting on one of the lobby's couches. A teenaged daughter of a middle manager, a graduate student doing her internship at the company, and a cubicle drone in his mid-thirties each occupy a cushion. But the cushions might as well be deserted islands for all the contact among the three of them. They sit facing forward, heads bowed. And all three are tap-tap-tapping away on their cell phones, completely disengaged from one another and from the conversations happening around them and from good old Bing dreaming of his white Christmas.

Ask yourself if you've ever seen this behavior. (Or perhaps, ask yourself if you've ever engaged in this behavior.) Now ask yourself if you think the three couch dwellers in the illustration are being antisocial. "Yes" is a perfectly acceptable answer: of course, they're being antisocial. All those folks around talking, laughing, carrying on. So many conversations to join and eggnog bowls to hover around, and those three sit in a corner glued to their cell phones! Didn't their parents raise them better?

If this is your reaction, I heartily agree with you, but take a moment to view the situation from another angle. Perhaps these three aren't being antisocial. Perhaps they're being (and I'm

8

about to make up a word) *trans-social*. They may not be interacting with the bosses, employees, spouses, and creepy mailroom guys who inhabit the lobby during the Christmas party, but they are conversing with (possibly multiple) friends via text message. They are checking up on what their friends are doing and where they are doing it via Facebook and Twitter.† They are being social—just not with the people close at hand.

At its broadest, trans-social behavior consists of socializing with people across a distance that makes face-to-face contact difficult. Of course, this has been around as long as there have been methods of delivering messages from one person to another: smoke signals, the Pony Express, and long correspondence like you find in Jane Austen novels. But as anyone who has read *Pride and Prejudice* knows, there's an awful lot of anxious pacing around sitting rooms and garden paths during the excruciating period between letters. So beginning with telephone calls and eventually continuing with e-mails, the Tech added a dimension of immediacy to trans-social behavior. No more anxious pacing— just an upbeat "You've got mail" from a digital voice. With the advent of online social networking in the last decade, the Tech has combined this immediacy with widespread distribution, thus providing the infrastructure for trans-social behavior to explode.

Let's turn back to our three trans-social folks and take a closer look. The teenager on Cushion One is updating her Facebook status with a rant about the creepy mailroom guy who keeps staring

---

† *Twitter:* A maximum of 140 characters can be sent at one time with the microblogging site Twitter.com. When this site went live, laconic people rejoiced. (btw, the preceding definition is six characters too long to tweet.)

at her. The intern on Cushion Two is texting with three of her friends and showing remarkable aptitude for keeping all three conversations distinct. The cubicle drone on Cushion Three is selecting the starting lineup for his fantasy football game against the friend of a friend whom he has never met in person, but with whom he has been messaging spiritedly about the game on the league's online forum.

The threesome sit on their respective islands, but it's no matter that the islands are deserted because they have open lines of communication to distant friends. They may be isolated in the physical world, but in the virtual world they find connections that bridge the gaps between deserted islands. We'll pick up the threads of connection and isolation in chapters 2 and 3; for now, let's think for a moment about the environment that the Tech has redesigned and the people like me who have never known any other environment.

We older Millennials (along with the last few GenXers) began blogging before *blogging* was even a word. On websites including LiveJournal and MySpace, we poured out all the mundane secrets, petty jealousies, and terrible poetry that used to belong to the private diary under lock and key. In the past, none of those words would have seen the light of day, but the Internet enticed us to divulge these confidences with an artificial promise of phony anonymity. Then older folks started warning us about our tendency to overshare on the Interwebs.[†] "If you put something

---

[†] *Interwebs, Series of Tubes, Internets*: All of these are nicknames for the Internet (the latter of which originated in a verbal gaff by former president George W. Bush at a presidential debate).

online, it can never be fully removed," they said. We adopted the appropriate shocked expressions until they went away, and then we joined Facebook and found a sleek new interface through which to bare our souls.

We extol the benefits of social networking: friends' birthdays right there on our profiles, reconnection with that old high school crush, the ability to organize a flash mob[†] to re-create the *Thriller* music video in the middle of the mall! But only in the last few years has the danger inherent in social networking begun to sink in: the inevitability of sexted[‡] nude photos winding up on the Internet, the ability for robbers to pick easy targets based on Facebook vacation updates, the omnipresence of cyberbullies online, and the data mining that follows every clicked link.

Social networking has enabled and amplified trans-social behavior to such a degree that all definitions of privacy are being rewritten. Until recently, private, direct, personal communication dominated; now it is giving ground to wide-spectrum, impersonal communication that may be private in nature but is public in disclosure. (Think about professional athletes who trash-talk over

---

[†] A flash mob is a group organized via social networking, which comes together at a certain time and place and executes some sort of (usually choreographed) routine such as dancing to a song from *The Sound of Music* in a train station. A late first-season episode of Fox's *Glee* (1.19, "Dream On") includes a good example of what a flash mob looks like.

[‡] *Sexting*: To text a nude picture of yourself to a boyfriend or girlfriend who has promised ("cross my heart and hope to die") that the picture will never leave that person's phone, which it will, of course. Sexting has resulted in charges of child pornography against the very teens who sent nude photos of themselves.

Twitter rather than on the field or court.) Indeed, the Internet is essentially a public place; however, to many of us Tech users, Millennials especially, it sure looks private because we interact with the Web while alone. For a Millennial blogger like me, I need to keep a personal journal in a physical spiral notebook just to be sure I keep myself from revealing things on my blog that aren't appropriate for public consumption.

The Tech has designed this public-disguised-as-private environment, and Tech users interact socially in this environment. What should be an individual's private identity often has public access enabled. The opportunities inherent in sharing socially across boundaries of distance are tempered by the dangers of ceding too much of oneself to the virtual world. Following Jesus Christ involves locating our identities first and foremost in the God who breathes those identities into our very souls. If we allow too much of our identities to escape into the ether of the virtual world, there may not be enough left to escape into God.

IN-GAME EXPERIENCE

The ether of the virtual world contains myriad places for us to spend our lives. Land may be a fixed commodity in the real world, but the capacity for expansion online is seemingly unlimited as server space continues to grow exponentially. As the Internet expands, the topography of the virtual map constantly shifts. Websites come and go. Online fads rise and fall. Web-based games exist as long as the publishers continue to infuse the games with new content. But even as the landscape of the Internet continues to change, the virtual world itself continues to grow. This growth comes in two forms. First, the expansive nature of the Internet caters to an ever-growing population of Tech users. Indeed, any statistic measuring worldwide Internet usage, which I could quote you on the day I'm typing this paragraph, would be meaningless by tomorrow, let alone by the time you read this book. Second, lightning-fast modern connection speeds have led to the growth of the immersive Internet experience. Not only is the Series of Tubes growing larger; the depth of experience available there is also growing. In fact, one can travel so deeply into the virtual world that it becomes difficult to find the way out. Here's what I mean.

When I was a nine or ten years old, I watched my father plug a telephone cord into the back of his computer, which ran a slick new operating system called Windows 3.1. He clicked the mouse a few times, and then he waited. The computer began making wheezy robot noises, and a few minutes later the screen flashed red. "Welcome to CompuServe," it read. My father let me take the mouse. I clicked it a few times until I found my first text-based adventure game. It was the kind of game that said, "You are in a dank dungeon. To your right is a bale of moldy hay. To your left is a locked door. Your inventory contains a piece of rope, a toothpick, and a flagon of mead." And then you had to figure out how to get out of the dungeon. There was a secret passage beneath the hay or else you bribed the guard with the mead. Whatever the text-based adventure, I was enthralled. I played the game whenever I could get my hands on the computer in the study. But the game was just a game—words scrolled down the screen, and I decided what to do based on a finite number of options and destinations. When I lost patience trying to figure out where to go next, I logged off and played with my LEGO bricks instead.

Fast-forward about thirteen years to the summer of 2006, and lo and behold, I'm still playing the adventure game. Except this time, my laptop's graphics card is working overtime to render seamless animation of staggering complexity. Distant mountains rise above the fog. Water laps against the moorings of a worn wooden pier. A boat noses against the dock, and a dozen creatures disembark. A bearded dwarf lumbers off the boat and produces a fishing rod and tackle. An elf somersaults down the pier and retires to an inn a few doors up the main street. A richly clad human conjures a steed from nowhere and gallops away. I wait for everyone to leave the boat, and then I climb aboard. My computer whines in protest—it knows firsthand just how difficult animating realistic water can be. The game that's taxing my laptop's graphics card is called *World of Warcraft*, which is shorthand for "the most successful and cunningly addictive online video game of all time."[†]

During the last week of June, a friend coaxed me into downloading the free trial of the game, and before Independence Day, I was hooked. Here's how it works. The player designs an avatar, which represents the player in the world of the game. The avatar is simply a computerized marionette, a virtual body through

_____
[†] Of course, "all time" is about twenty-five years. *World of Warcraft* is nicknamed *WOW* or *WoW*, as in, "WoW, you've been playing nonstop for nine hours. Don't you need a hot dog or something?"

14

which the player interacts with the fantasy world being projected through the Internet from the game's headquarters in California. The player can personalize the body of his or her avatar: elf or troll or dwarf; male or female; long hair, short hair, blue hair, no hair. With mouse-clicks, keystrokes, and typed commands, the player makes the avatar run, jump, fight, laugh, dance, or hurl fireballs.

This description may sound like a standard sketch of the average game, but I quickly discovered the difference between *World of Warcraft* and every other video game I had ever played. The fishing dwarf, the somersaulting elf, and the horseback-riding human were not simply artificially intelligent, computer-controlled characters set in *my* game to make *my* experience more real. Rather, they were the avatars of players like me. As they disembarked from the boat, they passed my avatar, another elf waiting to set sail.

Through the virtual body of my avatar, I interacted with the virtual bodies of hundreds, if not thousands, of other living, breathing people, who were connected to online servers from homes and dorms and coffee shops the world over.† The more I played, the more other players recognized me "in game." But they didn't really recognize me; they recognized Daeloth, the Night Elf rogue,

---

† The fact that, at any given time, hundreds of other people inhabited the same game world as I did makes *World of Warcraft* an MMORPG, which stands for "massively multiplayer online role-playing game." In the time since the game was created, more than eleven million people have played *World of Warcraft*. If I were still one of them, I'd have never found the time to write this book.

or Kementir, the Tauren druid. Adam was just the nebulous puppeteer on the other side of the keyboard, who began as a newb[†] and played long enough to become a crusty old veteran. Seriously, though, I played every available minute I had. There were days when I ate all three meals in front of my computer. There were always new quests, new levels, new accomplishments to keep me logged in. As the months stretched into a year, I disappeared deeper and deeper into my avatars. I neglected my diet, my exercise, my IRL[‡] friends. I fought and ran and flew in my virtual bodies while my physical body stagnated at my desk. My muscles and my creativity atrophied from lack of use. The game consumed me, and I was no longer Adam. I was Daeloth's player.

The Internet offers deep, immersive experiences, and I found mine in *World of Warcraft*. Unlike the text-based adventure games of my youth with their closely defined limits and linear construction, *World of Warcraft* takes place in a world of open possibilities. As in real life, the avatar works at professions, buys and sells at an auction house, eats and drinks, and spends time traveling and accomplishing tasks. As in real life, the game doesn't shunt players down carefully constructed linear progressions. As in real life, the game offers risks and rewards, boredom and excitement.

[†] *Newb* is short for "newbie," a rookie player who has no idea what's going on. This is distinct from *n00b* (yes, that is spelled with two zeros), which is an annoying veteran player who plays like a newb on purpose. (Some use n00b for both, but I prefer the distinction.)
[‡] IRL = in real life. (Here's a typical bit of *WoW* dialogue between players. Mightysteve, the Troll hunter: "What do you do IRL?" Dagron, the Undead warlock: "Oh, I'm a CPA.")

For someone like me, who in the summer of 2006 didn't like the way his real life was going, diving into the virtual world was just the escape I desired. *World of Warcraft* became my drug of choice as I sought to replace the failure of the real with the cheap and easy success of the virtual. I immersed myself in a world that the Tech made possible for me. I ignored my real life because the virtual one offered adventure, accomplishment, and assurance that life would be okay as long as I kept leveling up my characters.[†]

Of course, replacing real life with a virtual life programmed in California kept me from seeking adventure in the world beyond my computer screen. By consciously limiting my realm of interaction to that of the game world, I severely narrowed the field of places in which I might stumble into contact with God. When I logged on, I turned off the part of me that seeks God. I saw only the avatars of other players because everyone else was hidden behind a computer screen just like I was. But by God's grace, God didn't abandon me to the pixelated world of the game. Even in the virtual *World of Warcraft*, God encountered me on more than one occasion when I least expected to find God's presence.

The Tech expands the realms to which we may gain entrance, but it does so at the price of pieces of our flesh-and-blood lives. As we explore the opportunities and dangers inherent in the Tech, we mustn't overlook the fact that the virtual world and the physical

---

[†] *Level up*: The higher the level, the more skills you obtain. In *World of Warcraft* the level cap began at sixty. It was seventy when I stopped playing, was eighty during the writing of this book, and went to eighty-five between writing and publication.

17

world can coexist, but one can't permeate the other.[†] I can don armor and strap on a pair of daggers, but I can't step into the *World of Warcraft* and fight dragons. My virtual self exists not as flesh and blood and bone, but as computer-animated avatar and browser history and series of status updates. Seeking God in both the real and the virtual worlds makes us digital disciples. As we continue in this book, reflect on the virtual realms to which the Tech has enticed you to travel. Did you think to search for God there? Reflect, too, on the trans-social identity with which the Tech is redefining you. How is God present in that identity?

VIRAL PAUL

> Don't suppress the Spirit. Don't brush off Spirit-inspired messages, but examine everything carefully and hang on to what is good. Avoid every kind of evil. Now, may the God of peace himself cause you to be completely dedicated to him; and may your spirit, soul, and body be kept intact and blameless at our Lord Jesus Christ's coming. The one who is calling you is faithful and will do this. (1 Thessalonians 5:19-24)[‡]

As near as scholars can tell, Paul's first letter to the church in Thessalonica is the earliest surviving writing from the group of people who followed the way of Jesus of Nazareth. Before Paul wrote any of the other letters we still have; before the Gospel

---

[†] However, I'm still holding out hope for the invention of the holodeck of *Star Trek: The Next Generation.* Did you ever notice that when the cast wound up in some trouble on the holodeck, they couldn't get out and the holodeck's fail-safes always malfunctioned?

[‡] All biblical quotations in this book come from the Common English Bible (CEB); check it out at www.commonenglishbible.com.

writers penned the events of Jesus' life, death, and resurrection; before Jesus' followers were even known as Christians, Paul sent these words to the Thessalonians. Therefore, the passage above is a piece of the oldest extant trans-social communication in Christian history. And it has lasted down through the centuries because it went viral back in the first and second centuries.[†]

Paul wrote these words approximately 1,914 years before the original germ of the idea that became the Internet was scribbled down. And yet, as often happens in Paul's letters, his words provide us with eerily cogent and timely guidance for our Tech-driven world.

"Don't suppress the Spirit," he cautions. This is the Spirit who hovered over the face of the waters at the moment of Creation, and who descended on the disciples after Jesus' ascension, and whom Jesus sends to guide us "in all truth" (John 16:13). Paul's directive warns us against defining the set of conditions by which the Holy Spirit can speak to us. Anytime we develop new media or dream up new scenarios, the Spirit will be able to interact with us through the new things. This includes the Internet. We just have to pay attention.

But while we search for the Spirit in the new, Paul tells us, "Don't brush off Spirit-inspired messages." In other words, don't cast aside the words of the prophets, the old things that have guided you so well so far. The prophets spoke words of truth particular

---

[†] Well, at least the ancient world's version of viral, meaning it was recopied again and again and sent around to more churches than its original addressee. Basically, churches linked the letter to one another, thus unwittingly preserving it for us.

to their own times, but their words transcend particularity and continue to guide us today. Likewise, the Tech may have made everything flashy and fast, but there will always be treasures hidden away in musty volumes in the stacks of libraries, those vanishing jewels.

Allow the Spirit free range, and keep a grasp on the things that got you where you are, says Paul. Then, "examine everything carefully and hang on to what is good. Avoid every kind of evil." As I've said before and as I'll continue to say, the Tech, like most things in life, generates both opportunities and dangers. Paul counsels us to test all the things we are doing rather than blunder full speed ahead without looking at where we are going. How can we minimize the dangers while holding fast to the good opportunities inherent in the Tech?

With his words of counsel done, Paul prays for the Thessalonians: "May the God of peace himself cause you to be completely dedicated to him; and may your spirit, soul, and body be kept intact and blameless at our Lord Jesus Christ's coming." God created us to touch and to feel and to be aware of ourselves and of God. While we exist as part of God's creation, we cannot be the sons and daughters whom God created without that combination of spirit and soul and body. Indeed, Paul prays that these three be kept sound or complete. For the first time in the history of the world, the Tech gives us the ability to outsource parts of ourselves into mechanical contraptions. The Tech has changed the norm from face-to-face interaction to trans-social communication. The Tech allows us to spend our lives in virtual worlds that we can never fully inhabit. As we explore the effects of these new realities on us digital disciples, Paul provides us with good news at the end of his prayer. "May your spirit, soul, and body be kept intact and blameless at our Lord Jesus Christ's coming," he says. And then in all the fervor of hope, faith, and love, he finishes: "The one who is calling you is faithful and will do this."

2

FROM CONNECTION
TO COMMUNION

On Friday, October 22, 2010, the venerable old chapel burned down at the seminary where I studied to become a priest. Since the days before the telephone or radio began connecting people over long distances, the seminary has been bringing together students from near and far, and they have worshiped in that chapel. By the time I first walked through its heavy doors as a wide-eyed seminarian, thousands of other students had knelt and prayed and sung praises to God within the chapel's walls. As I knelt in a pew that day and took in the haphazard grandeur of a place that unabashedly combined various architectural and decorative styles from several periods, I could feel the prayers of those thousands give weight to my stammering efforts. For three years, I prayed in the chapel. I prayed with my friends and acquaintances, with guests and strangers, and with the great cloud of witnesses whose hushed voices made up the airy substance I felt that first morning.

The fire began around four o'clock in the afternoon. At a quarter to five, a friend called me with the shocking news. I logged onto Facebook, and the first thing I saw in my news feed was a grainy, thirty-second cell phone video showing the flashing lights of fire engines, a crowd of stunned onlookers, and flames leaping from the chapel's old wooden roof. By a quarter after five, I had received two e-mails and a text message about the fire. Every update of my Facebook news feed brought another shocked lament about the chapel. Spontaneously, students and alumni began changing their Facebook profile pictures to a photograph of the iconic east wall of the chapel: a stained glass window of Jesus commissioning his disciples bordered by words written in large black capital letters saying, "Go ye into all the world and preach the gospel."

Before the firefighters had finished snuffing the blaze, the community of students and alumni who had worshiped together for decades in the chapel re-formed online. All those who had for a day or a year or a lifetime called the chapel their spiritual home grieved together over the Internet. Friends, acquaintances, guests, and visitors met, and I am certain that the great cloud of witnesses penetrated the Tech and gave comfort to us mourners.

A decade ago, this kind of connection was impossible online. But the Tech has changed the game. We connect with more people, more quickly, and more frequently than ever before. On my Facebook news feed, I see my friends' statuses, and I see their friends' comments about those statuses. I navigate to Wikipedia and read an entry that one person wrote and dozens of others edited and supplemented. I feel hungry, so I open up Yelp on my iPhone and look for a Chinese restaurant nearby. I read several personal reviews that other folks have evaluated for accuracy. In all these daily occurrences, I am connected not just to one layer of other people but to many, the vast majority of whom I have never met face-to-face.

This ease of connection, this ability to link with countless others, offers to followers of Christ opportunities that a few years ago were far from the imagination. The Tech has generated an infrastructure for connection of surpassing breadth and depth. While it is true that most of the connections we make through the Tech are inconsequential and fleeting, the capacity for real, relational, and transformative connection—like the ones made on the day of the chapel fire—is abundant and growing. Following Christ through the terrain of the virtual world involves being aware of the presence of God encoded into this infrastructure and seeking out these deep connections.

NOW I'M NOT ALONE?

The twenty-year-old daughter of friends of mine moved to New York City for an internship between her second and third years of college. She had been savvy and independent for years, so my friends had no doubt that she could handle a summer in the Big Apple. She sublet a tiny apartment, settled in, and figured out how to take the subway to work. But a day later, on the verge of hysterics, she called her mother. She couldn't live here. She felt so isolated. In a city of eight million people, she was horribly alone! My friend listened and tried to console her as best she could, to little avail. A couple of hours later, the daughter called her mother back. Her voice neither quivered nor cracked. No hysterics, no snuffling, no tears. She was calm, composed, her earlier distress forgotten. "Are you okay, hon?" my friend asked. "Yeah, Mom," came the daughter's reply. "They turned on my Internet, and now I'm not alone."

From her little sublet piece of Manhattan Island, my friends' daughter reached across virtual space and connected transsocially with her friends in order to keep the beast of loneliness at bay. For someone brought up in the Tech-driven world, the impulse to reach out through trans-social connection was the default position: she found her solace through virtual contact. The Tech gave her the opportunity to stretch beyond the walls of that tiny apartment and gather her friends around her.

This impulse to gather holds the seeds of the religious life. This life begins with the urge to thank God for the simple fact that God created me. But this is just the beginning, because the next step in the religious life comes when I thank God for the simple fact that God also created you. While God created you and me to look ostensibly like discrete, individual units, God never intended us to function independently from each other. C. S. Lewis sees it this way: human beings "look separate because you see them walking about separately. . . . If you could see humanity spread out in time, as God sees it, it would not look like a lot of separate things dotted about. It would look like one single growing thing—rather like a very complicated tree. Every individual would appear connected with every other" (*Mere Christianity,* revised and amplified ed. [New York: HarperCollins, 2001], 180).

The impulse to gather derives from the knowledge that each of us has in the deep places of our hearts, which Lewis puts into words: we are all connected one to another. Religion is first and foremost about connecting with the God who makes all other connections possible. When we recognize that all connections happen through the binding and weaving presence of God, we set our feet on the path of the religious life. Followers of Jesus Christ make connections with God and one another by walking together along the path set by Jesus of Nazareth and expressed by his apostles.

In his life, death, and resurrection, Jesus revealed just how important the action of connecting is. He called his disciples to follow him and directed them to catch people as they had once caught fish. Rather than send the crowds away, he gave thanks, blessed, and broke a meager meal and fed more than five thousand people. He lamented over Jerusalem, saying, "How often I have wanted to gather your people just as a hen gathers her chicks under her wings. But you didn't want that" (Matthew 23:37; Luke 13:34). Even while suffering on the cross, he knit together a new family when he bound his mother and the disciple whom he loved to each other. In his resurrection, he showed us the utterly indomitable lengths to which he goes to remain connected to us; indeed, not even death severs the connection. The apostle Paul put it this way: "I'm convinced that nothing can separate us from God's love in Christ Jesus our Lord: not death or life, not angels or rulers, not present things or future things, not powers or height or depth, or any other thing that is created" (Romans 8:38-39).

The path we walk while following Christ connects us to one another and helps us see the truth that, though we may look like separate, individual beings, we are actually part of one great living body, whose purpose is to participate in the reconnection of God's entire creation back to God. Paul calls this the body of Christ, the members of which each has a different purpose but each proves indispensable to the functioning of the Body. When you and I discover how we fit into this great Body, we begin to move from connection to communion.

Connection happens when two or three gather. But connection turns into communion when, as Jesus says, "two or three are gathered in my name, I'm there with them" (Matthew 18:20). Connection recognizes the weaving movement of God in and through our lives. But connection turns into communion when we intentionally gather to celebrate that weaving movement. Thus, we participate in the weaving, in the communion, through our very celebration of it.

Communion happens when we show gratitude for the gifts that we have been given by using them to do God's work in the world. As members of the body of Christ, we have our special gifts, but most gifts come wrapped in the people around us. Just because we aren't good at some particular task doesn't mean we get to clock out early. It just means we have the opportunity to invite someone to help us. This is communion—celebrating God's blessing by connecting with one another to bring the kingdom of God just a little bit closer.

Believe it or not, this communion can happen online. Even in the virtual world, each small connection carries within it a seed of holiness, a prompting from the Divine to reach out and gather in. Each is a potential religious experience waiting to happen. My friends' daughter had no connections when she moved to New York City, and immediately the fear of isolation set in. But once her Internet came on, she was able to log back in to her virtual community. She reconnected with the friends who support and love her. Because she linked with her friends via a virtual platform, the limiting nature of *place* had no effect on her ability to connect. A snapped-in Ethernet cable or a strong wireless signal was all she needed to connect her and her community. The opportunity here for followers of Christ lies both in the extreme portability of connection and in the Tech's relegation of distance from the list of things that make communion impossible.

A couple of years ago, I heard a story that fascinated me. A woman died in a car accident and a funeral was arranged. Dozens of friends came to mourn her loss. They gathered at a snowy cemetery in Winterspring and shared stories about their deceased friend. This sounds entirely ordinary. But then you might ask, where is Winterspring? And this is the point at which the story becomes fascinating. Winterspring is a level fifty to sixty zone in the northern part of the continent of Kalimdor, which is part of the land of Azeroth, which exists solely in the virtual space of *World of Warcraft*. The in-game friends of someone who died in the actual world came together at a virtual cemetery to remember a friend, whose avatar would no longer venture in the world of Azeroth. These people lived all over the world, held various jobs, spoke various languages. But they all connected in the virtual world of the game. They created a virtual community at a virtual place, and I am convinced that God imbued their gathering with actual meaning. You see, even in the virtual world, communion happens.

THE NEW HOUSE CHURCH

I begin writing this section while delayed at Logan Airport in Boston. I perch on a window ledge and sweep my eyes over my fellow would-be travelers, each of us trapped between security and Jetway. The fingers of eight out of ten people are attached to some device or other. Mobile phones are most prevalent, followed by laptops and iPads. Everyone seems to be attempting to connect with a loved one or a coworker or an airline representative. I continue to look and listen. Snatches of frantic and exasperated phone conversations reach my ears: a canceled flight, a business trip running over by a day, a missed recital, a father trying to console a young ballerina from afar. I hold out hope that I'll still be able to make my connection in Baltimore, but with each further delay the chances dwindle. As the minutes wear into hours, I ruefully reflect on the several definitions of the word *terminal*.†

If the apostle Paul were alive today, I wonder whether he would have added "flight delays" to his catalog of hardships, along with imprisonments and shipwrecks. Paul went to great lengths to connect with the churches he founded, and thankfully, we have the written evidence of several of those connections. In the early days of Christianity, even before followers of Jesus appropriated the term *Christian* from their detractors, those followers met with one another in private homes. These house churches sprang up throughout Greece and Asia Minor as Jesus' disciples took seriously his command to "be my witnesses in

---

† I did make my connection, btw—four hours, three delays, two storms, and one pizza later.

Jerusalem, in all Judea and Samaria, and to the end of the earth"
(Acts 1:8).

When these early Christians gathered, they met at the house in
the neighborhood that could fit them most comfortably. The particular house had no special significance above its superior square
footage. When a house church grew too large, the congregation
split (one would hope amicably) into two smaller house churches,
and one of the groups began meeting at another location. The
place itself held little importance. The people were what mat-
tered. Indeed, when Paul addressed his first letter to the church in
Corinth, he didn't send the letter to a building with stained glass
windows and a bell tower with a cross on top. He sent the letter
to a gathering of people—a fairly messed-up gathering of people—but to a gathering nonetheless.[†] While individual house
churches shared many basic beliefs about God and Jesus, usually
instilled by a church planter like Paul, their relative isolation
encouraged a certain entrepreneurship in liturgy and theology.
(This is a reason that Paul sounds either angry or exasperated
fairly often throughout his letters.)

But as the church began emerging from its persecuted early
years, the house church declined in importance. Christians built
special houses, the only purpose of which was to provide a place
for Christians to gather and worship God. Skip forward about a
thousand years, and these special houses didn't really look like

---

[†] Paul uses the Greek word for "church" (*ekklesia*) twenty-one times in
his first letter to the Corinthians. I found that out using the Interwebs,
just so you know. Online Greek Lexicon FTW. (FTW = for the win; in
other words, "Yippee!")

houses anymore. The largest rose hundreds of feet into the air, supported by flying buttresses, adorned with masterfully wrought stained glass, and festooned with artfully carved gutter disguisers (better known as gargoyles). The idea behind these ginormous buildings was that you couldn't help thinking of God when you saw them. They were the church's ultimate home-field advantage; no one could stand in the shadow of their massive façades without feeling at least slightly intimidated. (And that's precisely what the church's leadership wanted.) With the ascendance of the dedicated church building—whether a one-room thatched establishment deep in the backcountry or a soaring cathedral visible from miles away—came the associated notion that "church" was a place rather than a gathering. This centralization of the church in specific locations helped the church's leadership standardize liturgy and theology throughout Christendom.[†]

Skip forward several hundred more years, and we're back in our Tech-driven world. Today, the church continues to exist as it has ever since it stopped being illegal to be a Christian (about seventeen hundred years ago, give or take a decade). Drive down any Main Street in the United States, and you'll count half a dozen church buildings. If they are anything like mine, the roof leaks, the carpet needs replacing, and there are too many sets of stairs for people with physical challenges to feel entirely welcome. Furthermore, every property committee meeting will be filled with anxious speculation about sources of funding to keep the

---

[†] Please forgive my woefully abridged survey of this specific aspect of church history. Of course, a lot of other stuff happened.

church in proper order. More often than not, this sort of speculation trumps the true purpose of church, which is to be a people gathered to worship God and serve one another through Christ's love. (A clever person once named this the "edifice complex.") However, in today's Tech-driven world, something new is also happening. Well, actually, the resurfacing of something old is happening. Alongside the church gathered in special buildings, people are also gathering in a new form of house church online. The democratizing force of the Internet allows people to come together in the name of Christ outside the four walls of a building. The extreme portability of the Interwebs allows people to meet regardless of their physical locations. And the Net's imperviousness to distance allows people from all across the world to meet in virtual space. Once again, *place* holds little significance, and the focus shifts back to the people gathered.

I am aware that this is a rather romanticized perspective of Christian gatherings online. Too often, Christians use the Web to spew vitriolic rants about the supremacy of single, inhospitable (and often hate-filled) viewpoints. Not wanting to encourage this sort of behavior, I've deleted multiple comments on my blog concerning my utter lack of things necessary to get into heaven. These comments are usually written in all caps and are never checked for spelling.

Putting this inevitable use for any form of communication aside, the Internet offers followers of Christ incredible opportunities to connect with one another apart from a concern for the edifice. The new house church meets when a thoughtful blog post spurs vigorous and amiable conversation about Jesus Christ. The new house church meets when a tweet links to a website exposing the plight of child soldiers, and the partner charity raises thousands of dollars as a result. The new house church meets when a prayer request goes out via a Facebook status update, and within hours three dozen people are praying for the friend in the ICU. Following Jesus Christ is about connection with God and with one another. The new house church—meeting on blogs, forums, and feeds across virtual space—connects the faithful to one another. And when we meet in the name of Christ, we discover that Christ is there as well.

A SPECIAL SORT OF ATTENTION

The more time I've spent online, the more I've had to develop my ability to notice the presence of God in virtual space. This kind of noticing is difficult because it involves practicing being especially attentive to the things that are always there. When I first moved to the coast of Massachusetts, the glory of the glittering morning ocean overawed me every day on my way to work. A mere five months later, I have to remind myself to look. And every morning, I am surprised that the gilded waves are just as beautiful as they were the first time I saw them. This is how our human brains work: with so much information downloading every minute into our neural hard drives, we tune out the constant things in order to see clearly the things that change. We perceive that the changing things will affect us more immediately, and so we grant them more consideration.

This perception affects all of us, and in the end, it hinders our ability to follow God as closely as we may. Like the ocean, God is a constant that we fail to notice most of the time. When we do attend to God's presence, however, we are surprised that we ever forgot to look. Practicing this sort of special attention is difficult in the real world, where we can deploy all five of our senses in pursuit of God's movement. But in the virtual world, where our senses are cut by 60 percent, this difficulty, like Spinal Tap's amps, goes up to eleven.

And so we must practice noticing God's presence. The first step in this practice is training ourselves to assume that God happens to be wherever we are. This is a safe assumption because God happens to be everywhere. In this case, "everywhere" includes the undefined "where" of the virtual world. (I don't have a very good reason for why I believe that God is in virtual space. I just have faith that God is there, which, I guess, is a pretty good reason.)

The next step is acknowledging that God's everywhereness is the very thing that hampers our ability to see God's movement. When we practice seeing the constant things in our lives (the ocean, the sky, our spouses†), we grow our ability to recognize God's constant presence. With the Tech changing rapidly and the Internets looking new every day, our neural hard drives fill up with these immediate things, leaving less room for noticing our constant God moving within and throughout all things.

The third step brings us back to the topic of this chapter. Remember, every connection holds within it a seed of holiness,

---

† Our spouses, you say? Yep—sadly. "He never looks at me anymore." "She always takes me for granted." These are markers of our human tendency to miss what's always there.

which is the potential to notice the God who makes all connections possible. In my experience, successful practice of God's presence online has derived exclusively from cultivating these connections and properly attributing them to God's movement. Perhaps you've discovered other ways to see God's movement in the virtual world. I haven't found them yet. Indeed, while I admit that computer graphics are absolutely incredible, watching a pixelated ocean roll in and out in the virtual world of an online game fails epically when compared with the real thing. Likewise, connecting with other people online is no substitute for face-to-face interaction (more on this in chapter 3). Unlike the pixelated ocean, however, a virtual connection between two people is still real because the people tapping away at their keyboards are living, breathing creatures of God's wonderful design.

Thus, the third step involves retraining our hearts and minds to rejoice at these virtual connections and see the movement of God behind them. God was present when my friends' daughter rejoined her online community and no longer was alone. God was present when the group met at the virtual cemetery in Winterspring to say farewell to a friend. And God is present in every ad hoc house church gathering on Facebook right now.

Review the connections you have made in the virtual world. God moved through them, but God's presence is constant, so you might have missed that movement. Because we spend so much of our lives online, we must be on the lookout for God in our virtual connections. Next time, practice noticing the presence of God.

Here's an example from my life to get you prayerfully thinking on the right track. In February 2010, I posted my fourth video

Bible study to my blog. A Presbyterian from Chicago, pseudony-mously calling herself "Noodles," commented on it. Tickled that someone I personally didn't know commented on the blog, I e-mailed her to thank her for her interaction with the material. That started a long chain of e-mails in which we talked a lot about God and a little bit about cheese. We became online friends, and a month later I mentioned to her that I (despairing that I would ever meet a datable woman by conventional methods) had joined a dat-ing website. She did not have a high opinion of the one that I joined, so she encouraged me to join a different one. I did, and the very next day, on this new site, I met the woman I would marry exactly one year to the day that Noodles commented on my blog.

As a follower of Jesus Christ, I do not believe in coincidence. I believe in God's connecting presence in the lives of everyone—in the real world and in the virtual one.

WON'T YOU BE MY NEIGHBOR?

A legal expert stood up to test Jesus. "Teacher," he said, "what must I do to gain eternal life?"

Jesus replied, "What is written in the Law? How do you interpret it?"

He responded, *"You must love the Lord your God with your whole heart, with your whole being, with your whole strength, and with your whole mind, and love your neighbor as yourself."*

Jesus said to him, "You have answered correctly. Do this and you will live."

But the legal expert wanted to prove that he was right, so he said to Jesus, "And who is my neighbor?"

Jesus replied, "A man went down from Jerusalem to Jericho. He encountered thieves, who stripped him naked, beat him up, and left him near death. Now it just so happened that a priest was also going down the same road. When he saw the injured man, he crossed over to the other side of the road and went on his way. Likewise, a Levite came by that spot, saw the injured man, and crossed over to the other side of the road and went on his way. A Samaritan, who was on a journey, came to where the man was. But when he saw him, he was moved with compassion. The Samaritan went to him and bandaged his wounds, tending them with oil and wine. Then he placed the wounded man on his own donkey, took him to an inn, and took care of him. The next day, he took two full days' worth of wages and gave them to the innkeeper. He said, 'Take care of him, and when I return, I will pay you back for any additional costs.' What do you think? Which one of these three was a neighbor to the man who encountered thieves?"

Then the legal expert said, "The one who demonstrated mercy toward him."

Jesus told him, "Go and do likewise." (Luke 10:25-37)

A legal expert is testing Jesus. Is this hubris? It seems that way to you and me because we know who Jesus is: asking questions of the Son of God always seems a bit bold. But this lawyer thinks Jesus is just a teacher, so let's forgive him his temerity and applaud him for serving up a juicy pitch, which Jesus knocks out of the park.

Funnily enough, the expert fixes on what he supposes will be a tough question: Who is my neighbor? However, Jesus isn't interested in *who* is a neighbor. Rather, Jesus wants to talk about a more life-impacting issue, namely, *how* this expert might be a neighbor to others. So Jesus does what he always does. Instead of answering the question in the form that is posed to him, he addresses the question he thinks *should* have been asked.[†] In this

---

[†] Jesus' unspoken rewrites of people's questions tend to be much deeper than the ones people ask him. This trend occurs throughout the Gospels: people never seem to ask the questions Jesus wants to answer.

case, Jesus recasts the lawyer's question. "Who is my neighbor" becomes "How shall I be a neighbor?" Notice that the original question has a one-word answer: everyone. Not known for a laconic style, Jesus tackles his own version of the question by telling a parable.

The story sets up like a modern joke: "A priest, a Levite, and a Samaritan walk down a road..." The legal expert and everyone else listening have heard this one before; of course, the Samaritan will be the victim of the punch line. And in truth, the parable is a joke, just not the kind that Jesus' audience is used to. Rather, the parable is of the "foolishness of God is wiser than human wisdom" variety (1 Corinthians 1:25). The Samaritan—the unlikeliest of the trio, the butt of other Israelite jokes, I'm sure—turns out to be the hero. The priest and the Levite are supposed to live by the words that the legal expert quoted from the Torah: "Love your neighbor as yourself." Instead, they offer no help to the dying man. But it's worse than that. They go so far as to cross the road so they come nowhere near him. Up to this point, the joke's not all that funny.

Then the Samaritan—this outcast, this second-class half-breed—comes along and takes care of the injured man. But it's better than that. He goes so far as to place the man on his own donkey, take him to an inn, and pay for his recovery. Now it's Jesus' turn to toss the fat pitch: Which person acted as a neighbor? This time the legal expert gets the gold star. He could have answered simply, "That unclean Samaritan"; rather, he reveals that he got the joke: "The one who demonstrated mercy toward [the dying man]."

The easy answer to the lawyer's version of the question is even truer in today's Tech-driven world. Everyone is a neighbor. You, gentle reader, and I have a much greater chance of meeting than people a thousand years ago, who lived in towns a mere twenty or thirty miles apart. You and I can connect with a few simple clicks and keystrokes.[†] So, with the easy question answered, we move on to Jesus' more difficult version. How can we be neighbors in the virtual world?

First, we recognize the ease by which we can mimic the priest and the Levite online. Severing a connection is as easy as closing a browser or deleting a bookmark. The Internet is a great platform for making these connections, but it's just as easy to travel alone through virtual space. In my *World of Warcraft* days, I often eschewed group play and soloed for hours on end. I took myself out of chat channels and ran around farming or completing KTB quests[‡] until my brain was numb. Like the priest and the Levite, I had to go out of my way to avoid encountering other people online. The potential for connection is just so darn ubiquitous.

Remember, though, it's more than mere connection that we are after. The Samaritan demonstrates his neighbor-of-the-year cred when he goes above and beyond the call of duty. Not only does he connect with the injured man; the Samaritan binds himself to

---

[†] Seriously, you and I are closer in our virtual neighborhood than I am to my actual next-door neighbors. More on this lamentable fact in the next chapter.

[‡] *Farming* is the term for collecting necessary materials for the making of other stuff. Very boring. Only slightly less boring is the ubiquitous KTB quest. *KTB* is the catchall acronym for a quest in which your character hunts a certain number of a certain type of creature. Not surprisingly, KTB stands for "kill ten bears."

the other man by serving him, by loving him. The Samaritan knows one of the great secrets of life, and Jesus shares it in this parable: there are never any strangers. Everyone is connected. But these connections are the mere seeds of something greater, and that thing is communion. Communion happens when we commit to transforming fleeting connections into lasting ones. Maintaining connections online until they blossom into communion is a tricky business because the Tech promotes inconstancy and change. But our God remains constant. When we notice the presence of God in our virtual connections, we can borrow God's steadfastness. And in the changes and chances of the Tech-driven world, we can be loving, constant neighbors, anchoring one another in the ever-shifting landscape of virtual space.

REMOTE INTIMACY

During my second year of seminary, I barely left my room. Besides attending class and (most) meals, I spent every other waking hour glued to my laptop. I had begun playing *World of Warcraft* the summer before, and by September I probably would have answered to "Daeloth"[†] more readily than to "Adam." We've already discussed how playing *World of Warcraft* affected my flesh and bones, so we won't go there again. But losing myself in an online fantasy world deteriorated not just my body, but also my relationships with all the flesh-and-blood people around me. While my friends played cards and watched TV in the dorm's common area, I sat alone in my one-window room.

But why should I have ventured outside Moore Hall room 203? Having a chat with a friend did not net me experience points.

[†] In case you're wondering how I came up with that character name, I combined two root words from J. R. R. Tolkien's Elvish lexicon found in the appendix of *The Silmarillion*. Daeloth was a stealthy rogue, and her name means "Shadow Flower." Go ahead and count the layers of nerdiness in this footnote. I dare you.

Tossing a Frisbee was not a quest objective. Going out to a celebratory birthday dinner did not level me up.[†] I was a citizen of a fantasy world, which offered a comforting mix of structure, repetition, challenge, and adventure. The quests overlapped, making it difficult to complete one without picking up a handful of others. Thus I kept playing and playing with the same "just one more" attitude of a drug addict. The rewards were tangible: a new sword or a new spell or a new piece of armor. I kept collecting virtual stuff and never noticed my devolution into the realm of narcissistic consumerism. And more than anything else, the feeling of leveling up was intoxicating. Oh, watching that golden flash illuminate my avatar felt good. How could the real world compare to this combination of purpose, prize, and achievement? The short answer is that for a long time it couldn't. And so, with a bag of pretzels in reach and a warm laptop on my knees, I isolated myself on the deserted island of my navy blue IKEA futon and played the game.

And for quite a while, I didn't notice my isolation. I noticed the headaches, which I told myself were the products of stress and MSG. I noticed the lethargy, which I told myself was a product of my taxing class load. And I noticed the twin spots on my laptop's casing, where hours of keeping my palms in the same place

---

[†] *Experience points*: Points you earn by killing monsters and completing quests. Earn a certain number and you gain a level. The higher the level, the more experience needed to achieve it. *Quest objective*: An NPC (non-player character) with a yellow question mark above his or her or its head gives you actions to do to complete a quest. Sometimes these can be as easy as "go talk to that guy over there." Most of the time they are much more difficult and/or time consuming.

literally wore away the silver color.[†] But I didn't notice the isolation because I didn't feel isolated. My avatars were surrounded by the avatars of all the other real people sitting on their IKEA futons around the world. We had textual conversations in chat channels. We talked through headsets. We were connected through the Series of Tubes. But that connection came at a price. At the same time that the Tech was connecting me to my in-game friends, it was also isolating me from those same fantasy world friends and from the friends down the hall.

I played *World of Warcraft* for a year. In July 2007, I quit for a host of reasons. But four months later, I relapsed and played for four more months during my senior year. I attempted to set limits for myself. They didn't work. Finally in March 2008, the flu sneaked up behind me while I was raiding a dungeon with nine other people.[‡] I told them I had to log off because I was going to be violently ill on my computer if I didn't. And I never logged back on. In the years since then, I have come to realize the inexcusable level to which I isolated myself from the flesh-and-blood people around me, all the while thinking that my virtual connections with the people in-game were sustaining me.

[†] Honestly. I gave that computer to a friend, but I bet he'd be willing to show you the spots if you ask him. I wonder if I'll gain a superpower from having absorbed that much silver metal into my skin. Can anyone lend me a surfboard?

[‡] *Raiding a dungeon:* In *World of Warcraft*, a raid is an organized event in which ten to forty people fill various specific roles in order to complete tasks throughout special zones called dungeons. Raids usually take several hours and draw the ire of significant others.

We've discussed the opportunities inherent in these connections, and I don't want you to think that the danger of isolation described here invalidates them. Remember, we can't separate the danger from the opportunity; we can only hope to trend toward the opportunity while trying not to ignore the nature of the danger. Most things in life present this kind of tension, and the Tech is no exception. But attentive followers of Jesus Christ live within this tension every day. Indeed, the very symbol of the Christian religion is an instrument of suffering and death, which Jesus redefined to be a symbol of hope and life. The cross is the ultimate reminder of the danger of separation, of abandonment, of isolation. But when the power of the Resurrection kept Jesus in relationship with us, even after his death on that cross, it has become a reminder of reconciliation, of union, of connection.

Connection and isolation are inseparable, especially in the virtual world of the Tech. How will we followers of Christ orient ourselves away from the danger of the isolation? We will explore this question in the chapters ahead. What is the nature of the danger? How does the Tech isolate us, and why do we fail to notice?

THE WALL

Think back to our trio of people sitting on their deserted island couch cushions during the Christmas party. There they are: one is updating a Facebook status, another is texting with three friends, and the third is selecting his fantasy football lineup. Around them swirl the sounds and smells of the company party, but they take no notice. An invisible but impermeable wall has twisted out of their cell phones and grown up around them.

This wall is the necessary by-product of trans-social behavior, and it exists in two ways. First, the wall separates the teenaged girl, the intern, and the cubicle drone from the rest of the party-goers. The three of them make no eye contact with anyone. They do not move from their cushions. And when they inevitably produce pairs of stringy headphones from their pockets and insert them into their ears, then good luck ever getting their attention. You might just have to produce your own cell phone and call them from across the room.

Second, the wall separates the three from the very friends with whom they are trans-socially interacting. Let's focus on each one in turn. The teenager updating her Facebook status broadcasts her thoughts on her profile. The news feeds of a hierarchy of family members, friends, and acquaintances automatically publish the new status. Some will read her description of the creepy mail-room guy and chuckle. Others will ignore the post. Still others will never know it exists because they rarely check their Facebook pages. The thought will be gone, buried under the next three hundred posts, by the time they log in. The girl projects her thought into the ether of virtual space, expecting that someone will read it and perhaps respond to it. She offers one side of a trans-social conversation, but she only knows that people have read her words when they comment on the status or click the ubiquitous link labeled *Like*.

The intern texting with her three friends has no opportunity to hear their voices. She can only see their words on the screen of her cell phone. They may use capital letters or emoticons or the omnipresent LOL to try to convey emotion, but these measures go only so far.[†] Therefore, the girl has difficulty interpreting the tone of the texts she is receiving. Predictably, the sarcasm in one friend's words fails to transmit in textual form, and the girl reads it seriously. The remainder of the texting conversation then revolves around clearing up the misunderstanding caused by the limitations of trans-social communication.

In an attempt to psyche out his competition, the cubicle drone selecting his fantasy team posts to the league forum some pointed comments about the poor skills of the professional football players on his opponent's team. The next day, his opponent responds in kind. The war of words rages back and forth. But their good-natured ribbing happens in fits and starts because one posts only after he notices the latest volley from his opponent. Thus they are separated not only by distance but by time as well. Their trans-social interaction never flows smoothly. When game day finally dawns and the rosters are finalized, the two opponents have accomplished the requisite trash-talking about each other's team. But the forum displayed their discrete units of trash talk fully formed in blocks of text. This is far from real, face-to-face insulting, which rolls off the tongue one derogatory word after another in real time.

[†] *Emoticons*: Otherwise known as smileys, emoticons rose to prominence during the heyday of AOL Instant Messenger. Back in the day, emoticons looked like these: :)   ;)   :(+<(:^) (the last one is a bishop). In other news, *LOL* stands for "laughing out loud," though anecdotal data suggest that the frequency of actual audible laughter to instances of the use of LOL is quite low. More often than not, people use LOL to denote that they do not want what they are texting to be taken seriously.

In each instance, the nature of the Tech itself causes the wall, which hinders the interaction between the three couch dwellers and their friends. The teenager, intern, and drone are isolated not only from one another (even though they are sitting within arm's reach), but also from the very people to whom they are connecting. For these fictional couch dwellers—and for many real people that you may know or that you yourself may be—trans-social behavior is the norm. The wall exists during every single texted conversation, virtual gaming session, Facebook rant, interoffice e-mail chain, online shopping experience, and all other trans-social exchanges. The wall is present during the majority of these folks' interactions, and so they feel comfortable behind it. For our trio, the Christmas party feels uncomfortable because face-to-face connection happens in real time between two or more present individuals, and it involves eye contact and interpretation of tone and body language. The wall precludes any of these realities in their normal, trans-social, daily lives; therefore, the three remove themselves from the immediate social situation and hide behind the wall of the Tech.

When we follow Jesus Christ, we walk behind him as he breaks down walls. In his life, he broke down the walls between healthy and sick, rich and poor, child and adult, Samaritan and Jew. In his death and resurrection, he broke down the walls between life, death, and new life. In his sending of the Holy Spirit, he broke down the wall between our blindness and God's movement. Because of this grace-filled work, we have the ability to walk down his path, past the rubble of these broken walls. Of course, apart from these walls, we set up many of our own, which we might not always want Jesus to break down. These walls stop us in our tracks, and they don't tumble down until we invite Jesus to take a sledgehammer to them. And then there is the new wall, the one erected by the natural limitations of the Tech. Those of us who spend most of our lives in the virtual world reside comfortably behind this wall. How can we help Jesus break this one down?

THE NEW HERMIT

We need Jesus' help breaking down the wall of the Tech because the wall isolates us. And any sort of prolonged isolation makes following Jesus difficult. We lose the support of everyone else who is trying to follow Jesus. And more important, we lose the opportunity to practice looking for signs of God's presence in the lives of those around us.

You've probably discovered this, but Christianity is a rather difficult religion to practice alone. During the days of the early church, certain devout Christians started the fad of going off into the desert to live alone as hermits. They thought that by denying themselves all worldly things, including other people, they could become closer to God. And for some of these ascetics, this plan worked swimmingly. But as the desert started getting crowded with people who jumped aboard the ascetical bandwagon, some of these hermits realized that they could become much closer to God by forming communities among themselves. They still practiced their frugal existence, but now they had friends to support them. Thus, the monastic tradition was born.

These early monks and nuns understood that isolation, while it may help clear the heart and mind of worldly clutter, does not fulfill Jesus' command to his disciples to love one another or Paul's directive to become the body of Christ. When we hide behind the wall of the Tech, we run the risk of isolating ourselves and taking ourselves out of the Body altogether. This happened to me when I lived in the world of Azeroth more than I lived in the real world.† And I didn't even notice. This is where the real danger comes in. We may not notice the isolation because we continue to feel connected to the people whom we meet in virtual space. But more often than not, these connections are transient and superficial. They stand in for real, meaningful human contact but fail to achieve it. They are like substitute teachers who turn off the lights and show videos because they don't know the subject matter. These facile connections do not trump the necessary isolation that arrives with them, and the more we rely on them, the more isolated we become.

Strangely enough, though these connections are transient and superficial, they often feel quite intimate. Speaking for myself, because I am safe behind the wall of the Tech, I have often felt comfortable sharing things about myself that I would not usually share face-to-face until deep into a friendship. The anonymity

---

† When playing *World of Warcraft*—if you type the command */played*—the game will tell you the aggregate time you have been logged in as a particular character. If you've played that avatar more than twenty-four hours, the game will begin counting in days—that is, full twenty-four-hour periods. My main three characters totaled several months.

makes the sharing easier because I know the other person doesn't *really* know me and therefore can't *really* influence me to change in any way. Furthermore, since the medium of the virtual world allows me to choose and edit my words with care, I am in less danger of accidentally saying things I don't want to say.

But because this intimacy always happens remotely, the connection between the two of us can progress only so far. I may know that you love the Decemberists, but I may never hear you sing along slightly, but endearingly, off-key to "The Crane Wife."[†] I may know that you love apple pie as much as I do, but we may never taste each other's concoction. I may know many things *about* you, but I will never truly know *you*. I won't know your laugh or how you prefer to hug or the peculiar way your bare feet make lopsided prints in the wet sand. Remote intimacy approximates connection the same way video games render the ocean. It may look realistic, but you can't jump in and splash around.

Remote intimacy creates the illusion of close relationship by focusing on what we like rather than who we are. When I joined the online dating site the day before I met my future wife, I filled out a profile of my likes and dislikes, and I tried to craft a few succinct paragraphs about myself. But what appeared on the site was a flat description of my appearance ("athletic" had a better ring than "skinny"), my iTunes library (the Decemberists et al.), my

---

[†] This is my favorite band, and my Facebook profile says so. But have you ever sat in the car with me and sung along? (Well, I imagine that everyone who has is reading this book; the other ten of you, look me up and we can take a drive.)

shelf of DVDs (Buffy, anyone?), my culinary preferences (mashed potatoes, of course), and the fact that God and I are pretty tight.

Thankfully, the bit about God piqued my future wife's interest, and she sent me a message the next day. I sent her one back, and for a few days we went back and forth. But having been in this situation before, I was conscious that we might develop remote intimacy, which could potentially hamper our ability to develop real, close, personal intimacy. You see, remote intimacy creates an avatar out of a real person. You add up data about that person but have no knowledge of the real, physical presence in which to store the data. The avatar is your own creation, a completely separate entity and often an idealized version of the original. In the end, you make friends with or fall in love with a virtual representation of a real person—one who suits your needs for friendship or love. Of course, the real person is much deeper, often more troubled, and always more vibrantly alive than the virtual avatar. He or she just isn't your version.

So, after one week of messages, my future wife and I met for tea and ended up talking for four hours. We never had time to develop remote intimacy, and our real, personal intimacy blossomed from the moment I almost knocked over the tea stand when I saw her.†

As followers of Christ, we may know many things *about* Jesus, but these things have limited potential to change our lives. Knowing Jesus himself can turn our lives around. More often than

---

† Clumsiness is something that rarely transmits over the Series of Tubes.

not, we meet Jesus in the lives of those around us. We meet him not when we simply know things about other people, but when we know them—when we know their doubts and tears and heartbeats. We were never meant to be hermits, isolated in the desert or isolated behind a computer screen. And while online connections have, by the grace of God, the opportunity to be real and true, every connection benefits from removing the wall. If you have remote intimacy with someone, consider meeting in person. Hear the timbre of his voice. Smell the citrus aroma of shampoo faintly clinging to her hair. Your remote intimates[†] will never be the people you made them into with your necessary virtual representations. They'll be better. They'll be themselves.

CYBERBULLYING, A TEST CASE

Ever since there has been school, there have been bullies inhabiting it. The stereotypical bully you might see portrayed on TV is bigger and stupider than other kids and usually wears some sort of frayed jean jacket. The bully takes lunch money with threats of physical violence or makes nasty and unverifiable claims about another kid's mother. And on TV, if the victim stands up to the bully, the bully quickly finds respect for his or her target and then

---

[†] Here's a quick (and possibly reliable) test for remote intimacy: change your birthday on Facebook to sometime next week (unless your birthday is actually sometime next week). Next, count the number of birthday wishes you obtain, and compare them with the number of confused messages you get from friends who thought your birthday was back in January. The people who sent the faulty birthday wishes are your remote intimates.

gushes about his or her own lack of self-esteem. In the real world, bullying isn't quite so one-dimensional. But real-world bullying does share one thing in common with bullying as seen on TV. It usually remains on school grounds, and at the end of the day, a bully's targets can scurry away to the safety of their own homes. Cyberbullying, on the other hand, follows a victim home from school. The Cyberbullying Research Center (cyberbullying.us) defines *cyberbullying* as "willful and repeated harm inflicted through the use of computers, cell phones, and other electronic devices." Victims endure the bullying whenever they use the Tech: she can't turn on her cell phone without getting texts filled with vitriol and hate; he can't log in to Facebook without seeing comments about his weight or hygiene all over his wall.[†] Someone sends her a link, which she follows to a website enumerating all the ways that she is a worthless human being; he discovers that someone hacked his account and bullied another kid using his name.

A 2010 report from the National Crime Prevention Council (NCPC)[‡] found that 43 percent of teens were the victims of cyberbullying in the previous year. The same report noted that 81 percent of youth said that others engage in cyberbullying because they think it's funny. It's not, of course. In the last few years,

---

[†] The Facebook wall is different from the abstract wall of isolation that I spoke of earlier in the chapter. A Facebook wall is a public area of someone's profile, on which others can post.

[‡] This is the group whose mascot, McGruff, told kids to "take a bite outta crime" when I was growing up. Does he still say that? You can find the full report at www.ncpc.org.

55

cyberbullying has been linked to multiple teen suicides, and perpetrators of cyberbullying have been expelled and have faced criminal charges.

The act of cyberbullying has reached pandemic proportions in part because of the danger we are discussing in this chapter: the wall of the Tech that isolates users of the virtual world from one another. Now, bullying has been around since one kid was bigger than the other. But schoolyard bullying and cyberbullying are vastly different things. The classic schoolyard bully has a size advantage over his targets. The typical "mean girl" is a popular power broker who has queen bee status. These two types of bullies are elite for one reason or another, and their power exists at school because of size or fame. They bully at school where their power lies, and therefore, they bully face-to-face, in the flesh. Cyberbullies, on the other hand, come in every shape, size, and level of popularity. The anonymity of the Tech grants the victims of "traditional" bullying the ability to bully the bullies. Therefore, the pool of potential cyberbullies grows to include everyone, not just the elites who dominate in the school yard.

These cyberbullies, most of whom would never fit the category of traditional bully, hide behind the wall of the Tech to accomplish their bullying. Some do it to avenge a wrong to themselves or to friends. Some do it just to be mean. Some do it because they are bored. In each case, the cyberbullying happens from behind the wall of the Tech. The cyberbully is isolated from his or her victim. Classic school yard bullying involves close connection between bully and target: an audible insult, a whimpering and timid defiance, a fist to the arm. The bully is forced to witness the effects of the bullying on the victim. But a cyberbully does not have to see the effects of his or her bullying. Writing "Everyone hates you and you should just die!" on a Facebook wall is as easy as reminding a friend to pick you up after practice.

The isolation between cyberbully and victim keeps the bully blissfully unaware of the target's mental state. Insulated from any consequences or feelings of remorse, the cyberbully keeps attacking. The wall of the Tech provides the perfect cover from which to launch the type of degrading salvos that the cyberbully would never think to say face-to-face. In fact, the NCPC's campaign against cyberbullying sports the motto: "If you wouldn't say it in person, don't say it online." Just the notion that McGruff has to remind teens of this basic human idea shows the extent to which the isolation of the Tech gives cyberbullies license to operate. This isolation is not only dangerous; it is potentially lethal.

LUKE, I AM YOUR FATHER

While he was still a long way off, his father saw him and was moved with compassion. His father ran to him, hugged him, and kissed him. Then his son said, "Father, I have sinned against heaven and against you. I no longer deserve to be called your son." But the father said to his servants, "Quickly, bring out the best robe and put it on him! Put a ring on his finger and sandals on his feet! Fetch the fattened calf and slaughter it. We must celebrate with feasting because this son of mine was dead and has come back to life! He was lost and is found!" And they began to celebrate.

Now his older son was in the field. Coming in from the field, he approached the house and heard music and dancing. He called one of the servants and asked what was going on. The servant replied, "Your brother has arrived, and your father has slaughtered the fattened calf because he received his son back safe and sound." Then the older son was furious and didn't want to enter in, but his father came out and begged him. He answered his father, "Look, I've served you all these years, and I never disobeyed your instruction. Yet you've never given me as much as a young goat so I could celebrate with my friends. But when this son of yours returned, after gobbling up your estate on prostitutes, you slaughtered the fattened calf for him." Then his father said, "Son, you are always with me, and everything I have is yours. But we had to celebrate and be glad because this brother of yours was dead and is alive. He was lost and is found." (Luke 15:20-32)

In this parable of Jesus, the father does all he can to remove the isolation that plagues his family. In the few verses before the above quotation picks up, Jesus tells of this father who has two sons. The younger son obtains his inheritance from the father, goes away, and wastes the money by living extravagantly. You might be tempted to think that his decadent lifestyle is his primary sin, but I'm not so sure. Rather, his major sin is the isolation caused by his separation from his family. Jesus makes a point to say that the father divides his household to fulfill his son's wish. And then the son doesn't settle nearby but in "a land far away." With the separation and isolation complete, all that's needed is a famine for the younger son to notice his folly. When he comes to himself sitting in the filth among the pigs, he realizes the isolation his departure caused. He no longer feels worthy to be called a son, so he prepares himself to live close to home but still isolated—a hired hand rather than a member of the family.

But his father has other plans. The father sees him coming from a long way off and runs out to meet him and embraces him and kisses him. "I am no longer worthy to be called your son," the young man says. But his father will not tolerate the isolation any longer. "This son of mine," he says, "was dead and has come back to life! He was lost and is found!" *This son of mine.* With these words, the father removes the isolation, and the two are reconciled.

The father throws a party to celebrate the younger son's return. His elder brother hears the revelry coming from the house and asks a servant what's going on. When he finds out about his brother's return, he will not enter the house or join the party. The elder son echoes his brother's sin by isolating himself from the celebration. When the father comes out to plead with him, the elder son shows the wall he has erected between himself and his family. He calls his brother "this son of yours," thus ignoring their fraternal relationship.

But the father continues to remove the isolation marring his family. "Son," he calls his elder boy. There is no wall between them because "you are always with me, and all that is mine is yours." Then the father attempts to heal the fraternal isolation by emphasizing the sons' relationship to each other: "This *brother of yours* was dead and is alive. He was lost and is found."

Both sons isolate themselves from the family, the younger by taking his inheritance to a land far away and the elder by refusing to join the celebration. But their father goes out, climbs over the walls the sons have built, and meets them in their isolation. He runs up to the younger son when he is still far off. He leaves the party to be with the elder. When neither brother feels much like a son, the father practices reconciliation and repairs the isolation defacing his family.

Isolation is a dangerous thing for us humans. It keeps us from forming close relationships. It allows us to hurt one another without noticing the damage we are causing. But God is in the business of bringing us back together. Like the father in the parable, God passes through the walls we set up and meets us in our isolation. The wall of the Tech, behind which we reside while living in the virtual world, is just another wall that God passes through. The question is: How will we respond when we notice that God is present on our side of the wall?

4

EMPTY MINDS AND DISPOSABLE BODIES

I've died several thousand times. I've been shot, stabbed, stomped, gored, eaten, burned, poisoned, cursed, and electrocuted. I've also drowned, suffocated, fallen from great heights, and blown myself up with poorly thrown grenades (the latter of which I've done with much more frequency than I care to admit). And you know what? I always come back. I might have to jog in spectral form to my prone body or repeat a portion of the level, but I come back nonetheless.

Video games have succeeded in making death cheap.[†] Every time I misjudge Mario's leap, and the innocuous little Goomba

---

[†] You might be tempted to dismiss this observation because the only people who play video games are guys with glasses and hygiene problems. But that's not the case anymore. Video games are as mainstream as movies and TV. The FPS *Modern Warfare 2* sold 4.7 million copies on its first day near the end of 2009. (btw, *FPS* means "first-person shooter"; in other words, it's a genre of game in which the player views the action through the eyes of the character. Oh, and the character shoots things with guns.)

walks into him, Mario dies. But his life total simply subtracts one, and I get to try again. Every time I forget to take cover, and the aliens pepper Master Chief[†] with plasma projectiles, he dies. But he simply "respawns" at the last checkpoint, and I get to try again. Every time I commit grand theft auto, and I start mowing down grandmas with the hood of my virtual Camaro, they die. And I keep driving as if nothing happened. And that's exactly the point: nothing did happen. No consequences. No repercussions. No cold, no rigor, no sightless eyes. No death.

In the virtual world of video games, death is a strategy rather than a conclusion. Death is part of the experience, not the end of it. With no physical, single-use, decomposable body to worry about, the player often allows the character to die in the course of deciphering the best way to accomplish a task. And game designers display this cavalier attitude toward death for good reason. To be sure, the commercial success of a video game that stopped working after a character's initial demise would be less than stellar. But danger exists when this cavalier attitude transmits through the games' mechanics to the players who wantonly dispose of their characters again and again.[‡]

Of course, I'm not the characters I play in video games. I can't double in size or throw fireballs with the help of the variety in my vegetarian diet. I can turn neither invisible nor invincible. I have a physical body that sweats and cramps and sleeps. And one day,

---

[†] Master Chief: The protagonist of the *Halo* trilogy, a grizzled marine trained as an elite soldier known as a Spartan.

[‡] It's possible that my views on this matter are colored by the fact that I die a lot in video games. I'm really not all that good at them.

my body will stop functioning, and I will die. Once. And that will be it for me on this planet. Until I die, this thought will be no more than an abstraction, I know. But I can't help thinking that every time I die in a video game, those cheap deaths are subtly eroding my awareness of the finality and physicality of my own bodily death.

The Tech removes physicality from the equation. In other words, whenever we use the Tech, it disembodies us. It eliminates the need for us to engage our bodies and, for that matter, our minds as well. Existence in the virtual world happens with no more bodily movement than fingers tapping on keys or game controllers. Employment of the Tech's vast and readily available stores of information happens with no requirement to file that information in the brain for later use. The Tech takes the mind and the body out of the starting lineup and replaces them with its own impervious virtual versions of us, which come complete with factory-issued virtual brains filled with all the information the Internet can hold.

The problem for followers of Christ comes when we remember that the Word didn't become machine or virtual presence. Rather, "the Word became *flesh* / and made his home among us" (John 1:14, emphasis added). The truth that Jesus Christ became a person—a living, breathing, thinking person—frames every expression of faith in the God whom Jesus makes known to us. When we allow the Tech to shelve our bodies and minds—the very things that God the Son emptied himself in order to inhabit—how readily will we be able to perceive and integrate God's presence into our lives?

The disembodying nature of the Tech brings us back to the intersection between connection and isolation, only this time the Tech isolates us from ourselves. Because of its external nature, the Tech naturally devalues the mind and body; it projects an illusion that the former is superfluous and the latter disposable. Followers of Jesus Christ know that the Word became flesh in order to help us find within ourselves the image and likeness of God, which is God's original gift to us. But when the Tech isolates the functions usually ascribed to our minds and bodies and programs those functions into external sources, accessing the image and likeness of God within becomes very challenging indeed.

OUTSOURCING THE MIND

You might hear the argument that adapting to the Tech is the next step in human evolution. But with every evolutionary step forward, something is lost (the vestigial tail, walking on all fours, the ability to spell). Usually, evolution takes a long time—what scientists refer to as geologic time because they measure it by looking at descending strata of rock. This lengthy period of time gives organisms and ecosystems some breathing room during which to adjust slowly to the adaptation. Those things that organisms lose over time as they interact with other organisms and with their environment are things that hinder their ability to be the fittest of survivors. Therefore, the loss is ultimately good for the species.

In the case of the last few Tech-driven decades, the evolutionary moment has taken very little time at all. Indeed, scientists might refer to this as "VH-1 time" because they can measure it by studying the series of fluffy television programs dedicated to low-wattage celebrities saying what they "heart" about various decades. With such a compressed period of adjustment, we haven't had the advantage of that geologic breathing room, which usually accompanies a change in a species. Therefore, we haven't had the time to weigh the potentially deleterious effects of adapting to the Tech against the benefits of thriving in this Tech-driven world.

Purely unscientific anecdotal evidence tells me that I used to be able to remember all of my friends' telephone numbers. Then I purchased a cell phone, began storing those numbers in a hard drive other than my brain, and now I can barely recall my own number, let alone anyone else's. While this example is less than serious, I can cite others that paint a bleaker picture: the cashier's powerlessness to count change without the computer telling him the amount. Or the student's impatience in failing to research past a subject's main Wikipedia article. Or my friend's inability to find my house on her third or fourth visit without the use of her GPS.

Although this evolutionary metaphor doesn't extend to the genesis of an entirely new species of hominid (*Homo interwebs* perhaps?), this anecdotal evidence demonstrates that the classification *Homo sapiens* is becoming less and less accurate. As I store more of both my memory and my capacity to solve problems outside my own mind, the "wisdom" (*sapiens*), which marks me as a member of the human race, withers and dies. For example, "wise man" shouldn't need his phone's calculator app to figure a 20 percent tip. But using the calculator is more convenient and less taxing on the ol' gray matter, so I take this path of least resistance. The next time the server drops the check on the table, I pull out the phone rather than engage in a few seconds of mental math. It's no matter that all I have to do is move a decimal and then double the number: I've lost the will to attempt the computation in house. So I outsource the responsibility of tip figuring to the device in my pocket. I repeat this method several times, and pretty soon, I've lost not just the will but also the ability to calculate a tip.

Again, the inability to figure a tip is a rather innocuous example, but it points to the alarming trend of preferring external sources over our own minds when we need to analyze, navigate, calculate, and remember. This trend has been picking up steam over the years as the Tech has shrunk in size, grown in capacity, and gained lightning-quick speed. For many people today, especially Millennials like me, employing the Tech to store information and to solve problems seems as natural as breathing. But this outsourcing of the mind diminishes the brain's capacity to do the things God created it to do. We can *find* answers to questions using the Internet, but the *ability* to question, the willingness to think critically, the desire to expand the mind and engage the cognitive process—these fundamental human characteristics are approaching their expiration dates.

As these characteristics of *Homo sapiens* come to the end of their shelf lives, the facility and yearning to engage the mind with the heart and spirit in contemplation of the Divine are the next things to go. Truly, the more we outsource our capacity to think and remember, the less capable we are of discerning God's call in our lives. We spend our entire lives sifting through the torrents of external stimuli, so how do we continue to pay attention to the still, small voice of God within each of us?

As we speed forward at the pace of VH-1 time, we tend to ignore the danger inherent in outsourcing our minds because the opportunity to save time and energy using the Tech is just so appealing. But along with this outsourcing comes the devolution of our minds and imaginations, both of which are necessary if we hope to follow Jesus Christ as closely as we can. Take the case of Jesus' parables, for example. The stories are simple on the surface: they tell of farmers and banquets and travelers on the road. Of course, Jesus uses this apparent simplicity to draw us in. His parables are like the ocean. You can stay on the surface and see quite a bit of blue expanding outward in every direction. Or you can dive down and discover worlds you never imagined existed. Jesus speaks in parables to force us to use our imaginations, to learn things about him and about ourselves that we could never find with a Google[†] search. Parables hold no easy answers. In fact, Jesus tells them precisely when people are looking for easy answers.

The Tech, on the other hand, is built for providing just such answers. One way for followers of Christ to combat the outsourcing of our minds to the Tech's effortless memory storage systems is to distinguish between information and knowledge, a topic to which we now turn.

[†] *To google*: To search the Internet using the Google.com search engine. This verb was added to the *Oxford English Dictionary* in June 2006.

KNOWING BY HEART

Back in elementary school—third grade perhaps—my teacher assigned the task of learning the poem "In Flanders Fields." If memory serves, the organizers of a Veterans Day event tapped my class to recite John McCrae's famous stanzas during the ceremony. I spent a week memorizing the poem line by line:

> In Flanders fields the poppies blow
> Between the crosses, row on row,
> That mark our place; and in the sky
> The larks, still bravely singing, fly
> Scarce heard amid the guns below.
> (*In Flanders Fields and Other Poems*
> [New York: G. P. Putman's Sons, 1919], 3)

I knew this first stanza best. I could say it in my sleep. The other two stanzas were a bit shaky, but I could get through them with a smidge of prompting. Veterans Day came, and my teacher anxiously asked the class if we knew the poem by heart. People had used this expression before: Sunday school memory verses, the Pledge of Allegiance. I understood that "know by heart" is another way of saying, "Do you have the poem memorized?" Sure, I told him. I know it by heart.

I memorized the words in the right order. The rhymes all fell in the correct places. The short-order cook in my mind laid the stanzas out on the counter ready to be served. Along with the rest of the class, I recited the poem, and then promptly, I forgot it. The poem was simply information that I downloaded into my brain. I never interacted with it. I never appreciated the incongruity of the lark's song and the gun's boom. I never noticed the heartbreaking tribute to the fallen, who from their graves urge us not to let their sacrifice be in vain. Of course, I was only nine. Even still, I memorized the poem and never once took the time to allow the words to invade my consciousness. I memorized the bits of information that made up the poem, but I had no knowledge of it in my heart.

In the decades since I memorized "In Flanders Fields," the Tech has championed the former side of this dichotomy. Information, rather than knowledge, reigns. The Internet is a collection of great storehouses and distributors of information. From its databanks, the Tech transfers information into the smaller hard drives of our brains. But once the transmission is complete, the Tech makes no demand that we then internalize the information. The data remain on the servers, ready for retrieval the next time around; therefore, we have no motivation to retain the data. Then the information just washes away and never has the opportunity to sink in and become knowledge.

Knowledge, on the other hand, is information that has the opportunity to burrow into our consciousnesses. Knowledge happens not through memorizing, but through knowing by heart. It happens when we interpret, analyze, struggle with, sleep on, and internalize information. Gaining knowledge is a slow process in which discovery of the external world and discovery of our own internal selves mingle to form our unique constellations of thoughts, feelings, and perspectives.

That being said, the Tech and knowledge are not necessarily strange bedfellows. All we need do is use the Internet for what it's best at—offering information—and then ignore the fact that the information will be available the next time we need it. Instead, we can store it in our own internal hard drives rather than on the external server. Then the information will have the chance to become knowledge.

For followers of Christ, the problem of storing information outside ourselves can lead to a diminished capacity of knowing our Lord and Savior. When the Tech conditions us to go through life utilizing single-serving packets of information, we have no practice searching our interior selves for the knowledge that only experience and reflection can provide. Previously, I mentioned the difference between knowing Jesus and knowing *about* Jesus. We can learn a great deal of information about Jesus, but until we make the commitment to internalize that information, knowing Jesus himself is much harder.

Armed with awareness that the Tech removes the obligation to store information within, we can practice generating knowledge by borrowing information and not giving it back, like the overdue library book that now resides on the shelf in the den. The less we outsource the mind and the more we practice deepening our capacity for knowledge, the better we can know Jesus by heart.

OUTSOURCING THE BODY

Music used to come on thin shiny discs, which you had to handle carefully for fear of scratching the exterior and making the data unreadable. True story. You'd get in your car, drive to the store, buy the compact disc, get back in your car, and then spend an agonizing twenty minutes trying to remove the plastic wrapping and adhesive labels so that you could listen to the CD on your way home. Once you got home, you'd pore over the liner notes, trying to decipher what in the world Dave Matthews was singing in the second verse of that one song. The CD would remain in the car for a while, and then you would store it in the bulging binder that ran out of room last year when you bought Dave's previous album. If the CD really lost favor, you might even relegate it to the milk crate at the back of your closet.

Nowadays, music comes on...well, nothing really. You turn on your computer, open up iTunes, click the link to the iTunes store, listen to snippets of songs, and then click *Purchase*. The music transfers from a server somewhere through the Series of Tubes and onto the hard drive of your computer. There's no plastic wrap to chip your fingernails on. There are no adhesive labels to make your fingertips sticky. There's no *thing* at all.

Music used to be encoded in the grooves of vinyl albums, written into the spooled tape of cassettes, and etched on the mirrored faces of CDs, but today's recordings need no tangible delivery system, no physical unit to read with needle or laser. If your computer suffered from Spontaneous Melting Hard Drive Syndrome, would your music survive? Are there milk crates full of dusty CDs in your closet? Do you back up your hard drive? If the answer to these questions is no, then chances are it's *hasta la vista*, music. Downloaded music offers no permanence, no physical presence, no ability to go rummaging around until you say, "Ah, here it is." The Tech has, in a sense, disembodied music.

The same is true for those of us who spend much of our lives online. Besides our key-pressing fingertips, our physical bodies

71

are removed from the equation.[†] The Tech disembodies us: our virtual lives happen outside the realm where our personhoods—those unique combinations of thought and creativity and flesh and blood—can affect much of anything. Here's an example.

Let's say that you and I haven't communicated in a while, so I decide to send you an e-mail. I type several paragraphs, add my name, and hit *Send*. The message travels through the Net, and the next time you open your e-mail you see Inbox (1). The message appears in twelve-point Arial font, the paragraphs are neatly justified, and the line at the bottom simply reads—*Adam*. Now, the content of the message may point to the fact that I typed it: perhaps I used an inside joke from that lunchtime when we were juniors in high school, or else I called you a nickname that only I can get away with calling you. But absolutely nothing else about the e-mail is unique to me. The thoughts that I put into words, which appear in twelve-point Arial font, have no connection to the body whose mind thought them.

Now imagine that instead of typing you an e-mail, I decide to write you a letter. I scrounge up some old stationery and scrawl out several paragraphs. The margins are irregular, as is the twelve-point Adam font, which is nearly illegible. My letters angle the wrong way, and I've smeared the ink in several places, showing that I am incurably left-handed. The telltale impressions of the words from page one raise relief on page two, demonstrating the heaviness of my hand. My clumsiness gets the better of me at the end of page three, and I stain the right corner with Earl

---

[†] What about our ears and eyes, you say? Good point—we'll get to them in the next section called "My Two Senses."

Grey. I sign my name to the left of the tea stain: the big, angular *A* connects through the middle letters to the little *m* that trails off into a squiggly line segment. I post the letter, and when you receive it, you receive not just the content with the inside joke and the nickname, but something written unmistakably by my body— a piece of my personhood, of my illegible hand, an offering of *me*. The Tech disallows this fusion of thought content and living bodies. Even our voices—those unique combinations of breath and pitch and vibration—are fading away as the Tech replaces audible communication with the generic and inexpressive medium of texting. We input our thoughts into devices that homogenize them and desaturate them of all that made them uniquely ours. Our words cease to be connected to ourselves. This is troubling for followers of Christ, for we believe that God created us as whole persons, whose bodies, minds, souls, and spirits work in concert to reflect the beauty of the image and likeness of God. God created us as whole persons, but we have broken ourselves, and in our brokenness, the reflection is dim, fractured. There are myriad ways to be broken, God knows, but only recently has the Tech made it possible for us to be broken through desaturation and disembodiment, which come as necessary side effects of spending our lives online.

For centuries, certain devout Christians have sought to deny their physical bodies in order to exist more readily on a spiritual plane. These folks often fasted to the point of malnourishment or whipped themselves to show that their bodies had no power over them. In these acts, they were, in a sense, attempting to disembody themselves because they believed the body to be a hindrance to their ultimate spiritual goals. With the advent of the Tech, we disembody ourselves not for the lofty aim of coming closer to God; rather, disembodiment is a symptom of our current way of life.

But our bodies are not hindrances. Nor are they just the biotic pieces of our increasingly cyborgian culture. Our bodies are vessels of the spark of God's creativity, which resides in each of us. This spark interacts with each of us uniquely, making every individual a one-of-a-kind creation of God. Our brokenness conceals the spark: we live our lives oscillating between trying to uncover the spark and attempting to hide from it.

One person in all of history, however, lived with the spark completely unconcealed. Jesus of Nazareth lived a life full of God. This life attracted people who had nothing figured out and repelled people who had everything figured out. Jesus welcomed with abandon, healed with compassion, and spoke with authority. He spoke the words of God, and not only that—he was the Word of God incarnate.[†] Before Jesus became a human person, he existed as the Word, through which all things were made and all of creation came into being. And because God loved the world so much, God sent this Word to us. The Word became flesh and lived among us in the person of Jesus Christ. God's Word around which all creation is organized became a particular, individual, grimy, hairy, dusty, beautiful human being.

Jesus' life was quite fleshy; indeed, his incarnation brooked no half measures. He was hungry and tired and angry and grief-

---

[†] *Incarnate*: This means to become flesh, to become a body. Look at the middle of the word. You know how *carnivores* eat meat; well, in*carn*ate comes from the same root in Latin.

74

stricken and dozens of other emotions that prompted physical, embodied reactions. He looked people in the eye, spat on the ground, drew in the dust, broke bread at table, tended fires, touched people with leprosy, and washed feet. In this life of feeling and speaking and loving and healing, Jesus embodied abundance and wholeness. "I came so that they could have life—indeed, so that they could live life to the fullest," he said (John 10:10). His life full of God shows us how to live our lives full of God. I am convinced that this fullness spreads to the virtual world of the Tech, but it does so at the cost of physical embodiment. So how do we who often exist in virtual space make up for the loss of these bodies, into which God breathed life and planted the spark of creativity? How do we trend toward the fullness that Jesus offers us when we use the Tech, which necessarily diminishes our capacity to live as incarnate beings?

MY TWO SENSES

I'm sure you've noticed that it's impossible to smell things through your television. The liberal application of perfume, the wet dog, the decomposing body—none of these potent smells transfers from the glowing boxes in our living rooms to our olfactory senses. In fact, we know that these odors affect the show's characters only because we (a) see them cover their noses in disgust or (b) hear them mention what a rotten smell is coming from so-and-so. I know this is terribly obvious, but take just another few seconds to think about it. To convey the notion that a *smell* affects a character, the audience must either *see* or *hear* evidence of the aroma's presence.

The Tech may have come a long way in the last few decades, but sensory perception on the Interwebs and other media continues to be limited to a mere 40 percent of our available senses. I can see video on the screen, and I can hear audio through the speakers. But taste and touch and smell? These three senses are always conveyed through a mixture of the other two.[†]

Therefore, during the time I spend in the virtual world, the Tech never stimulates three out of my five senses. When my avatar eats an apple pie, I can't taste the tartness or smell the aroma of baked crust and cinnamon. When I video chat with a friend in need of consoling, I can't wrap her in an embrace. Whenever I choose to spend my life online, I limit my God-given faculties for the length of my virtual session. I impair myself like those folks whom Jesus heals in the Gospels, except that they don't have a choice in their physical challenge and I do.

Furthermore, the two senses that the Tech does allow me to use are mere facsimiles of the originals. No matter how much depth I can see on a screen, the image is always an illusion presented in two dimensions. And no matter how many speakers surround me, the audio always projects from discreet places at fixed distances from me.

[†] For as long as there has been video, there have been folks trying to get the sense of smell involved. From the short-lived Smell-o-Vision to scratch-and-sniff cards, none of these attempts has really worked out too well. If you head to Disney World, you might see an attraction that uses smell—otherwise, you're out of luck. Also, video game systems introduced the "rumble" feature in the mid-1990s. The controller shakes when certain things happen; however, when getting tackled by a linebacker and getting shot in the face produce the same generic vibration, one can see how this is a less than satisfactory analog to the tactile sense.

Knowing that sensing life in a virtual setting can match far less than half of that in the physical world, I constantly remind myself of the need to stimulate all of my senses. I can see and hear the ocean from where I am typing right now. But to rehabilitate the three senses that I've long ignored, I walk down to the water and smell the baked-seaweed smell of low tide. I taste the salt in the air. I dig my bare toes in the wet sand and feel the surf swell around my ankles. While I can deceive myself into thinking that the Tech can provide all the sensory input I need, one minute on the beach truly shatters the delusion.

Like undergoing my oceanside rehabilitation, worshiping God in a communal setting gives me the opportunity to engage all of my senses. I hear voices rise in song. I see the preacher talking with his or her hands. I smell the old incense still clinging to the carpet. I touch the hands of my neighbors when we offer one another the peace of the Lord. And I taste the gifts of bread and wine, which through blessing, breaking, and sharing have some-how become the body and blood of Christ.

These are sacramental acts—sensory experiences that allow me to participate in God's movement in the world. The sacramental action of worship nourishes me to go out into the world to per-form other sacramental acts such as feeding and clothing the poor, building houses for the homeless, and visiting the lonely. Following Christ involves living sacramentally, and living sacra-mentally always involves the body, both my own and the greater body of Christ to which I belong. The more time I spend living online, the less time I have to be a living sacrament in the world.

That being said, God has an uncanny way of permeating our

entire lives, both physical and virtual. While the Tech limits my senses by 60 percent, it makes up for the limitation by extending the remaining senses far beyond my feasible range of movement. And God gives me the ability to project my heart across those distances even through the feeble facsimiles of sight and sound. During my *World of Warcraft* days, I often found myself in conversations about God and faith with the real people behind the avatars. We'd be fighting off bands of wolves or perhaps gathering keys off ogres, and God would enter our conversation. To paraphrase the Gospel According to Matthew, whenever two or three avatars gather, Christ is there.

THE INCARNATION AND THE INTERNET

In the beginning was the Word
and the Word was with God
and the Word was God.
The Word was with God in the beginning.
Everything came into being through the Word,
  and without the Word
  nothing came into being.
What came into being
through the Word was life,
  and the life was the light for all people.
The light shines in the darkness,
  and the darkness doesn't extinguish the light....
The Word became flesh
  and made his home among us.
We have seen his glory,
  glory like that of a father's only son,
    full of grace and truth. (John 1:1-5, 14)

John begins his account of the gospel with this beautiful poem. God spoke creation into existence. With God's Word, all things came into being. Life—physical, embodied life—came into being. And in due time, this Word, which was God and was also with God, became flesh. The Word became the body, which we know as Jesus of Nazareth. We examined this Incarnation earlier in the chapter, but let's look a little closer. First, imagine this scenario with me.

A man signs up for a blogging website and begins creating a blog. He calls his first post "The Kingdom of God Has Come Near." Another blogger stumbles onto his website. "This blog is much better than mine," says the second man, and he directs all of his subscribers to check out the new blog. The first man uploads a post called "Follow my RSS,"† and within a few hours, he has several subscribers. He continues to post, and more people start reading his blog. The original subscribers don't quite understand everything he writes, but they still read all of his posts. The blog starts attracting the attention of people who disagree with the man's ideas. They post vehement comments on his website, mostly in all capital letters. Soon, the government takes notice of the man's writing and finds it seditious. They sever his connection to the Internet, but a few days later, the man hacks back online. He sends e-mails to his original subscribers, telling them

---

† RSS is the acronym for a certain type of Web syndication; in other words, RSS helps you collect lots of Web-based things that update with regularity. The acronym has been around since 1999, but the words that RSS stand for have changed several times (RDF Site Summary, Rich Site Summary, Really Simple Syndication). RSS also stands for the Royal Statistical Society, which is a professional body for British statisticians. (That's not important for this footnote, though they do sound like a smashingly interesting group.)

that he is logged in again, but that he needs them to spread his message over the whole world. They begin blogs of their own, and pretty soon these new blogs go viral. Websites about the man begin popping up all over the Internet.[†]

If Jesus were alive today, would his ministry look like this? Would he be a relatively unknown blogger who made the wrong people angry? As far as I can imagine, this is the closest contemporary analog to his ministry in Galilee and Jerusalem. Seems a bit humdrum, doesn't it? Something is definitely missing.

That something is the Incarnation, the belief that God loves us so much that God's Son became one of us so that we might learn to become more like God. The Word didn't pretend to become a human being. Jesus wasn't a vision or a divine hologram. God the Son was born in a human body, which walked and washed, ate and drank, spoke and held its tongue, lived and died. Jesus embodied a life full of God and invited those around him into that life.

Nowhere is this clearer than in John's phrase translated above as "made his home among us." The translators did the best they could rendering this phrase into English; sadly, it still loses all of its vigor when it's removed from its natural Greek habitat. In the original language, this phrase literally means "to pitch his tent among us." In a culture steeped in the story of the Hebrew people, John's audience would read this as an allusion to God's presence with the Israelites as they wandered through the desert for forty years. They set up a special tent, which housed the holiest

---

[†] Please understand that this thought experiment is not intended to devalue Jesus' actual ministry. I'm simply trying to make the point that Jesus' physical presence was fundamentally necessary for that ministry.

relics the Israelites owned. [†] They believed that God, who created everything, dwelled especially in that tent. By pitching the special tent everywhere they went, they assured themselves that God continued to be with them, no matter their status as homeless wanderers. This understanding of God was quite different from other contemporary cultures, whose gods were tied to specific places. The special tent was the primary reminder for the Israelites that God was everywhere.

So, when "the Word became flesh," God pitched another tent to refocus the faith of God's people. In the physical presence of Jesus Christ, John and all of Jesus' followers saw "his glory, / glory like that of a father's only son, / full of grace and truth." They followed not an abstract idea or notion, but a person, who loved them and taught them how to love.

The stories of Jesus healing people show the beauty of his Incarnation, of his human embodiment of the Divine. Although Jesus practices long-distance healing on a couple of occasions, the majority of his interactions with those who are ill or physically challenged happen at close quarters. Jesus heals a man who cannot hear by putting his fingers in the man's ears, spitting, and touching the man's tongue. Jesus makes mud and smears it on the eyes of a man born blind. Friends of a paralyzed man dig a hole in the roof and lower him down so he can be close to Jesus. This closeness, this skin-to-skin contact, this healing of the physical body, warns us of the dangers of letting the Tech disembody us.

[†] Indiana Jones found the relics in 1936, and then the Nazis stole them from him. But God wasn't pleased and melted the Nazis' faces off. At least, that's the way the film tells it.

Of course, Jesus no longer has that physical body, and so you might wonder why all this talk of embodiment is important in a world infused with God's Holy Spirit, who is inherently disembodied. The fact that Jesus no longer has a body makes our continued embodiment vital. We are, as Paul tells, the body of Christ. Each one of us has the opportunity to participate in the Incarnation by embodying Christ in our own lives. To live sacramentally means to take every chance to display Christ in our speech, our service, and our love. If nothing can separate us from the love of God in Christ, then sacramental and virtual living cannot be mutually exclusive. The question is: How can we embody Christ in a disembodied world? The spiritual practices described in the next two chapters help me answer this question. They help me stay connected to God even when I find myself in the isolation of virtual space. By working hard to maintain this connection, we can still be parts of the body of Christ even in the virtual world.

5

GOOGLING PRAYER

While I was brainstorming this chapter (otherwise known as "procrastinating on Facebook"), I clicked a link from a friend's posting and stumbled across the fascinating Beloit College Mindset List.[†] The creators of this list originally intended it as a humorous reminder to their fellow professors not to assume that incoming students would understand their cultural references. With lists dating back to 2002, the catalog has become a world-renowned chronicle of rapidly changing recent history. I read the list for the class of 2014 and discovered that, contrary to what my author bio says about me, I may not have my finger on the pulse of the Tech generation. Alas, after comparing the current list with the list for my college class of 2005, I seem to be approaching antique-hood—at the ripe old age of twenty-seven.

[†] Check it out for yourself at www.beloit.edu/mindset/2014.php. If you graduated from college in 2002 or later, there is a list for your year. The best one on the list for my graduation year is this: "They have probably never used carbon paper and do not know what cc and bcc mean." So true. I didn't know what "bcc" meant on my e-mail until a few months before I wrote this footnote.

In the list for my class of 2005, the professors needed to be reminded that "a browser is not someone relaxing in a bookstore; a virus does not make humans sick; and a mouse is not a rodent." Of course, no such lexicon accompanies the list for the class of 2014. At the beginning of the 2000s, the vocabulary of the Tech—let alone the Tech itself—had not yet saturated the culture. Nowadays, needing to be told the primary definition of *browser* seems laughably archaic. The speed at which innovation descends into antiquarianism is staggering: in today's Tech-driven world, relevancy is measured in months rather than decades.

And what's more, the very definition of speed is changing. When my class of 2005 was packing for college, the new mindset list advised that my peers and I "have always had access to e-mail." Less than a decade later, the current list notes that "e-mail is just too slow, and [the class of 2014] seldom if ever use snail mail." Now, let's be honest: e-mail, which is faster than Usain Bolt running the hundred meters, is not slow. However, in the world of today's matriculating frosh, it is *too* slow. They have been sending text messages since they received their first cell phones in elementary or middle school, and as means of communication go, texting is technically faster than e-mailing. While e-mails sit in inboxes waiting to be accessed, text messages demand attention the moment they arrive. Furthermore, the seconds one spends opening a mail program, addressing an e-mail, and clicking *Send* are superfluous in a world where the text message reigns supreme. Because they've lived their whole lives immersed in the Tech, members of the class of 2014 can tell the difference between immediate and really-super-close-but-not-quite-immediate. Thus anything slower than instantaneous is not fast at all.

For followers of Jesus Christ, this expectation of immediacy that the Tech makes possible can adversely affect our relationships with God. The immediacy of today's world can cause me to question whether God can keep up. If Google responds to my search in 0.17 seconds, why does God seem to take so glacially long? When I search the Internet for the answers to mundane questions, I can usually find them straightaway, so why can I never find answers to the "big" questions? With information so rapidly accessible outside myself, how do I remember to store knowledge of God within? When the media are more concerned with speed than depth or accuracy, what's around to influence me to live my Christian life deeply and permanently?

Following Christ may have an immediate beginning; indeed, the disciples followed Jesus "immediately" when he called them to leave their nets. But whether we meet Christ in a rush of immediacy or in a long, slow courtship, our daily walking with Jesus happens not in minutes, but in moments—glorious indefinite moments filled with God's presence. These moments are neither fast nor slow nor *too* slow; they just are. Whenever we feel hurried and harried by the Tech and our instantaneous world, a glorious indefinite moment with God is always waiting to happen.

Take a moment now, and then keep reading to see what I mean.

SEVENTY-SIX MILLION PRAYERS

The Google search took all of 0.17 seconds. I googled the word *prayer*, and in less than two-tenths of a second, the search engine returned 75,900,000 hits. That's a lot. If I were to spend one minute viewing each hit and not sleep and also not die when I'm supposed to, I would visit the last one sometime in November of the year 2154. Whenever I have a question or need to find something, I just google it. Can't remember the names of the original Power Rangers? No problem. (1,730,000 hits; 0.18 seconds.)[†] Need to find a picture of a 1967 Blue Ford Mustang? Simple. (162,000 hits; 0.30 seconds.) Whatever I need, Google seems to be able to provide it and provide it in less than half a second.

A part of me sure wishes God were that responsive. I say my prayers, I ask God for things, and I wait and I wait. But with Google returning millions of answers to my queries in the blink of an eye, prayer seems so slow. Of course, the questions I put to Google are of a different order than the ones I put to God, but the rapidity of the Tech is most definitely taking its toll on my expectations. In the years since the Tech has reached its current lightning-fast speed, I have come to expect everything quickly. I have come to expect everything at my fingertips. And I have come to expect everything to be packaged in small, digestible bites. Indeed, the worth of things is derived less by their value and more by the ease with which people can access them. Because I have grown up saturated in the Tech, I am conditioned to expect quick, easy access to information.

[†] Just in case you're wondering: Jason Lee Scott (Red), Kimberly Hart (Pink), Zack Taylor (Black), Trini Kwan (Yellow), and Billy Cranston (Blue). Tommy Oliver (Green) was bad to start out, but then he joined up after being freed from a spell. Yes, I was ten when this show premiered.

On top of this ease of access, the Tech is built specifically to respond to my needs: I need to know where I'm going, and so the Tech provides directions using the GPS software on my iPhone. I need an outlet for my creativity, and so the Tech provides a place to publish my writing using a blogging website. I need people to affirm me as a person (but not be so close that they might influence me to change for the better), and so the Tech provides them via social networking.

Humanity has spent its entire history creating systems designed to meet its needs: the false gods of wood and stone in the Hebrew Scriptures, the class system, slavery. But never has a system reached the pervasive coverage of the Tech, which is in the process of rewriting the human code so that we depend on it for everything. And whether I like this new code or not, it affects my relationship with God. If the Tech is built to respond to my needs, then shouldn't God be built for the same purpose? Furthermore, God seems so much less responsive than the Tech, so why should I bother with God at all?

And right here is where I notice how the influence of the Tech has led me astray. From the time God formed me in my mother's womb, I was never meant to exist primarily for myself. I was meant to exist for God. The Tech might be attempting to rewrite my code until I believe I am a king at my keyboard, isolated from everyone, yet with the world at my fingertips. But God is the original writer of the human code, and no matter how much reprogramming I undergo, that base code still operates uncorrupted. From within me, God continues to whisper that God does not exist to respond to me: I exist to respond to God.

Responding to God in my life is my primary purpose. Another word for response to God is *prayer*. This expansive definition of prayer comprehends more than simply listing requests before God; while this form of prayer is one valid expression, prayer itself is so much more. In its broadest definition, prayer is anything I do in response to God's initiating activity in my life.

C. S. Lewis describes this understanding of prayer in the narrative of *The Silver Chair*, one of his *Chronicles of Narnia*. The story begins with Eustace Scrubb and Jill Pole trying to escape a mob of bullies at their ghastly boarding school. From an insecure hiding spot, Eustace looks at Jill and wonders aloud if they might be able to escape to That Place. He begins calling out, "Aslan, Aslan, Aslan!" Jill follows his example: "Aslan, Aslan, Aslan!" The bullies discover the hiding spot, and Eustace and Jill scramble up a steep slope. The weathered old door in the wall is always locked, but this time the knob turns. And the two children step into Aslan's country.

They find themselves at the top of an impossibly high cliff. Eustace falls off the cliff when he tries to pull Jill back from the edge. But a lion arrives just in time and blows Eustace to safety in the land of Narnia. Frightened of the lion, Jill tries to slip away, but the great beast begins questioning her. Her showing off caused Eustace's fall, she confesses. For that display of pride, the lion gives her a task to perform. "Please, what task, Sir?" asks Jill. "The task for which I called you and him here out of your own world," says the lion.

This response puzzles Jill. Nobody called them. They called out to—Somebody—a name she wouldn't know. Weren't she and

Eustace the ones who asked to come? "You would not have called to me unless I had been calling to you," says the lion, who happens to be Aslan, the Christ-figure of Lewis's prose.

"You would not have called to me unless I had been calling to you." These words capture most profoundly our relationship with God. God never ceases to call out to us, and our response to that call shapes our lives as followers of Jesus Christ. In a world where the Tech exists to respond to our needs, listening for the call of God in our lives offers an escape from the reprogramming we are undergoing. If the Tech exists to respond to us, and we exist to respond to God, perhaps we can redeploy the Tech to serve God.

Rather than search for the names of the Power Rangers, search for information about a marginalized people and discern a way to help them. Use the Series of Tubes to find a charitable organization that helps a cause for which you have a passion. Connect with people on the other side of the world through a microgrant site and help fund small business in depressed developing areas. Find an online daily devotional, and use the Internet to deepen your relationship with God.

God calls to us in the real world and in the virtual world. We would be unable to pray if God weren't first calling to us. Our prayer—our response to God—is neither quick nor easy, but it can help us navigate the quick and easy avenues of the Tech. If you notice yourself being programmed with the quick and easy expectations of the Tech, try this: find a breath prayer that works for you. Maybe it will be the Jesus Prayer: "Lord Jesus Christ, Son of God, have mercy on me, a sinner." Maybe it will be a piece of St. Patrick's Breastplate: "Christ be with me. Christ within me." Maybe it will be something as simple as "Thank you, God." Pray your breath prayer every time you search the Internet. I don't know about you, but if my prayers equaled my Google searches, I would have a much closer relationship with God. Jesus promised that those who search will find. As we search using the Tech, I pray that we find the God who continues to call to us.

✳ A SPECIAL KIND OF TIME

In our Tech-fueled instantaneous world, everything happens faster than it used to. And yet, we never seem to have any time at all. One would think that with quicker transmission of data and more effective communication, we would save several hours a day, which people used to spend waiting around for things to happen. However, rather than save those hours, we inject them right back into our routine. We have become busier without realizing it, because our busyness is both more efficient and more portable. The division between office and home no longer exists with quite so defined a separation. Work follows us around in our pockets, buzzing and pinging and ringing and clamoring for our attention. When we aren't demonstrating our Pavlovian response to our smartphones, we spend time playing mindlessly repetitive games on Facebook or searching YouTube[†] for the best videos of people crashing their skateboards. The Tech efficiently sucks away

---

[†] *YouTube.com*: The largest video-sharing site on the Internet, specializing mostly in home movies with poor sound and lighting. My current favorites are the literal music video of "Total Eclipse of the Heart" and the videos of the guy who does sign language to pop songs.

all of our busy time, and directly afterward it sucks away all of our free time as well.

And so we never seem to have any time to spare. Every minute, Google adds 247.5 bytes to a mailbox's storage capacity. Every hour brings more ways to tell the same tired story on the twenty-four-hour news cycle. Every day needs a fully charged cell phone. The Tech opens the floodgates of information, and we spend all of our time attempting to process the deluge.

The trouble for followers of Christ is that Jesus calls us to live outside this kind of frenetic, overscheduled, minute-speeding-after-minute conception of time. When Jesus says, "My time hasn't come yet" (John 7:6), he uses a special word for time that has less to do with the clock than you think it might. The word he uses would be used for the time when you eat dinner not because it is the dinner hour but because you feel hungry. This special sort of time is baseball game time, in which innings take as long as they must. It is "once upon a time" time, expectant time, the kind of time in which unfulfilled promises meander toward completion. It is time mixed somehow with eternity, which still slips away but in no predictable way—time that will come when it needs to.

This is the sort of time into which Jesus calls us to live and move. When Jesus invites us into his time, we discover again and again the ultimate reality that most good things are worth waiting for, are worth working for, are worth anticipating. Jesus' time is measured in breaths rather than seconds, in moments rather than minutes. These moments are the times when we stop and notice. They are the times when the beauty of one particular rain-drenched daffodil or the rattling discord of a homeless veteran's

Styrofoam begging cup catch us up and leave us breathless, stricken by joy or sorrow or, more often than not, a combination of both.

The Tech has no concept of this kind of time. But we followers of Christ do, and we have the ability, with God's help, to remain in Jesus' time even when we engage the Tech in our daily lives. In the next chapter, we'll discuss a small selection of practices that will help us enter this special kind of time. But for now, if you find it difficult to let go of the instantaneous nature of today's world, even for a few moments, try this: sit down and take several deep breaths. Close your eyes and turn your attention inward. Keep breathing slowly, deeply. Without using your hand, see if you can feel your heart beating against your chest. Take as much time as you need. Get quiet and then get quieter still. Focus on that steady, dull squeeze. Feel it? This is where the rhythm of Jesus' time resides in us.

THE WEDDING READING

> As God's choice, holy and loved, put on compassion, kindness, humility, gentleness, and patience. Be tolerant with each other and, if someone has a complaint against anyone, forgive each other. As the Lord forgave you, so also forgive each other. And over all these things put on love, which is the perfect bond of unity. The peace of Christ must control your hearts—a peace into which you were called in one body. And be thankful people. The word of Christ must live in you richly. Teach and warn each other with all wisdom by singing psalms, hymns, and spiritual songs. Sing to God with gratitude in your hearts. Whatever you do, whether in speech or action, do it all in the name of the Lord Jesus and give thanks to God the Father through him. (Colossians 3:12-17)

I realize that I've been very much down on the Tech in this book. The more I write, the more I discover just how much the Tech has influenced my life for good and ill. But when we come right down to it, I don't think the Tech is bad or wrong. I think it is simply another thing we humans have made using our God-given gifts of ingenuity, intellect, and creativity. But like nuclear power, which can fuel houses or destroy them, the Tech is both beneficial and destructive. The more aware we are of the dangers, the more we can move toward the benefits.

With this constant thesis of the book once again firmly in our minds, I confess to you that I could not find a suitable passage for this Bible study. I looked and searched and prayed, and nothing fit. Then I received a text from my fiancée (yes, the one I met online), who was on her way to shop for bridesmaids' dresses. This made me remember that we chose these words of Paul for one of our wedding readings. I share them with you because they succinctly describe how we are best able to trend toward the opportunities and away from the dangers of the Tech (and of marriage, for that matter). And I share them with you because Paul tells us to "teach and warn each other."

Paul says, "The word of Christ must live in you richly." Remember this instruction during every search of the Internet. We mustn't let information we gather leach out of our minds' soil. Tend it. Cultivate it. Let it take root and become knowledge. Knowledge nourishes the soil and makes it rich; ideas grow and flourish. In the midst of this flourishing, we can find the word of Christ within. And it will live in us richly and nourish us.

Paul also says, "The peace of Christ must control your hearts."

Remember this direction as the world flashes by too quickly to keep up. Jesus resides in a special kind of time that infuses our minutes and hours with the boundless quality of eternity. When we notice Jesus tugging us into this kind of time, we find peace, the peace that controls our hearts. Tethered to Jesus' time, we clock our lives in moments and allow the peace of Christ to rise within us as we move through our instantaneous world.

Paul finishes his thought with these words: "Whatever you do, whether in speech or action, do it all in the name of the Lord Jesus and give thanks to God the Father through him." Remember this wisdom when prayer seems too slow and God seems unresponsive. We are capable of speaking and acting, of browsing and downloading, of texting and googling because God continues to breathe life and Spirit into our bodies and souls. Therefore, in everything we do, we either respond to God or disregard God. When we promise to live our lives in the name of the Lord Jesus, we pray for the ability to respond to God in all that we do. And God is faithful, which is why we, as Paul instructs, "sing to God with gratitude in [our] hearts."

6

TECH SABBATH

It is a wholly unremarkable evening in early August: bright, sultry, the air close and stale. The afternoon drizzle never amounts to anything, and the coals light just fine. I carry the shrimp and chicken sausage inside. My shirt smells like hickory charcoal. The four of us sit around the table—my fiancée, her sister, her brother-in-law, and me. We chat about nothing in particular. The meal passes pleasantly but unremarkably, like the evening.

Near the end of dinner, our conversation predictably falls to the topic that conversations among four late-twenty-something nerds often do. *Star Trek: The Next Generation* aired from 1987 to 1994, just in time to claim its role as our collective childhood dream-shaper. We begin discussing episodes of the series that take place on the holodeck, the virtual reality recreation area that, because *Star Trek* is science fiction, is more real than virtual. Several episodes feature characters pretending to be detectives: Data as Sherlock Holmes, Captain Picard as . . . as . . . as . . .

What was the name of Captain Picard's detective persona? The four of us are stymied. On the holodeck, he plays a PI from a mid-twentieth-century pulp mystery series. People wear trench coats and carry tommy guns in violin cases, and the street is always smoky and dark. But what is the detective's name? "We could look it up online," my fiancée suggests.

We look at one another for a few seconds, and then we reach an unspoken agreement. "No, we can figure it out," my future brother-in-law says.

"I think it's Dick," offers my fiancée's sister.

"No, Picard plays a dick, as in 'private detective.' His name's not Dick," I say.

"In my mind, I can hear the secretary say his name in her nasally voice."

"Yeah, she says a nickname, though."

"I can't remember."

"Is it something like Tex?"

"Dix?"

"Yeah. That's close."

"Dixon."

"Dixon Hill!"

We say the name and we know it's right, and for some reason, we all experience a brief moment of giggly catharsis. "Dixon Hill. Man, that would have bugged me for days," I say.

Except that it wouldn't have. After a few hours, if the question were still niggling and nagging at me, I would have searched for it on the Interwebs because that is what I do when I don't know or can't remember something. What makes this unremarkable conversation remarkable is the unspoken dialogue that passed among the four of us after my fiancée suggested that we look up

Picard's detective name: *This time we are not going to outsource our minds. This time we are not going to employ the Internet as our surrogate brain. We know that this small, completely insignificant piece of information is somewhere in those few pounds of gooey gray matter, and by golly, this time we are going to remember it.* Four Millennials, some of the eldest members of the generation, stifled the instinct to consult the Tech, and who knows, perhaps we cleared the brush and encroaching branches off some of our disused neural pathways.

Our giggly catharsis happened because we were, I think, unwittingly proud that we didn't jump immediately to the quick solution. If we had used the Series of Tubes, we would have found the answer perhaps five minutes sooner. Instead, we slowed down. We worked together. We engaged our minds. And we dredged up that bit of nerdy trivia.

We spend much of our lives in the instantaneous, disembodied, remotely intimate, trans-social world of the Tech. We move at broadband speeds. We interact through virtual bodies. We connect from a distance. None of these things is evil or inherently harmful. But when we reach a point that we never slow down or interact with our physical bodies or connect face-to-face, we are no longer living the life that makes following Jesus Christ the primary priority.

In the final pages of this book, we will discuss several spiritual practices that are far older than the Internet and the telephone and, for that matter, the printing press.[†] These practices come from a

---

[†] Well, a couple are roughly contemporaneous with the printing press, but you get the idea. They're old.

world where plow, scythe, and pitchfork were cutting-edge technology, but they have withstood the test of time. These practices have helped anchor me within the constant that is God, so that I am not swept away by the modern current of impermanence. I commend them to you. They will help us stop and take a few deep breaths in the midst of the whirlwind that is our Tech-driven world. Use them as you follow Christ in both the real and the virtual worlds.

A Place with No Bars

The ironic thing about writing this book is that I had to turn off my wireless access to the Internet to do it. If I did not click *Turn Airport Off*, I would inevitably follow one of my questions to Wikipedia and come to myself fifteen minutes later, wondering how I got from the history of the CD-ROM to ladies' pumps in four clicks.[†] Fairly early on in the writing process, I realized that if my editor were going to be holding the manuscript in his hands by our mutually agreed-upon deadline, I had to shut off the Interwebs.

And so I did, and I found quite a bit more time to write. These miniature, three-hour vacations from the Internet helped me focus on the task at hand and kept me from chasing every white rabbit that dashed through my mind. I was still using the Tech: my laptop

---

[†] In case you are wondering, go to www.wikipedia.org and search for *CD-ROM*. Then click *Optical disc drive*, then *Magnetic tape drives*, then *Shining shoes with a cloth*, then *Pumps*. Of course, thanks to the impermanence of the Series of Tubes, these links might not be active at the time you read this footnote.

lay open in front of me, ready for me to fill a blank document with words, and my cell phone waited for incoming calls over the 3G network. Even with the wireless disconnected, I was still connected, still plugged in and battery powered. Indeed, if, for some reason, the Feds needed to question me, they could track my phone's GPS transponder.[†]

Because I am always reachable, I never have the chance to allow myself a period of regenerative solitude. Jesus knew the benefits of this kind of retreat. When the crowds were hounding him day and night, he slipped away by himself or with a few friends for some alone time. He did his best praying and listening when he went off by himself, because hearing his Father was easier when the voices of people clamoring for his attention were far away. Following Jesus' example, I've found that, besides my three-hour vacations from the Internet, every once in a while I need to go, as a friend once put it, "to a place with no bars."[‡]

Every year since I was eleven years old, my family has traveled into the mountains of North Carolina to a place that AT&T doesn't know exists. For a week, we read books (actual books with musty pages and the potential for paper cuts!), enjoy each other's company while sitting in rocking chairs on the porch, and try our level best to stay lashed to the mast as the siren song of the wireless Internet in the main lodge calls to us. The week apart from the Tech reminds us that people lived just dandily way

---

[†] You know, because the FBI is always calling in crack investigative priests to help with its more difficult cases.

[‡] That is, bars of cell phone reception. I can't comment on the presence of bars that serve adult beverages.

back when there was no such thing as Facebook and when people knew where you were when they called you because your phone was attached to the wall of your kitchen. The week also provides the necessary inoculation to the remote intimacy that dominates our normal lives. Over time, we've realized that solitude is isolation with a purpose. It's like fighting a virus by making a vaccine out of the virus itself. Solitude helps us remember the importance of true, close, personal connection for the human experience.

Our week at a place with no bars is our Tech Sabbath. When we reenter the instantaneous world after a week of moving at the slow pace of pre-industrial society, we bring with us the knowledge that one cannot survive on Tech alone. Yes, we turn our phones back on and check our e-mail, but a small voice deep within keeps whispering that if I accidentally drop the phone in the toilet, it's not the end of the world.

My family has our Tech Sabbath all at once. I know other folks who observe a Tech Sabbath every weekend. For one day, the television, DVR, phone, computer, iPod, and all the other gadgets receive no power. This act brings them into the space of regenerative solitude, and they notice that their central nervous systems still function even with the Tech turned off.

If you can't ignore the ping of your smartphone's e-mail program for the length of your kid's Little League game, consider a Tech Sabbath. If you can't make it through a feature-length film without texting a friend about how boring/awesome/confusing the movie is, consider a Tech Sabbath. If you have difficulty dropping off the grid even for a few hours, consider a Tech Sabbath. I am sure, if Jesus were alive today, that he would at least put his phone in airplane mode when he went off to chat with his Dad.

YES, LORD, YOU ARE HERE . . .

If you open the top drawer of my bedside table, you will find a stack of college-ruled notebooks. Each notebook is filled with my mostly illegible handwriting chronicling the presence of God in my life and my mostly lackluster ability to be present to God during that life. The journal entries date back to 2006, when my spiritual director, a wise woman with flyaway red hair and holy eyes, prescribed for me a daily dose of specialized reflection based on St. Ignatius's "Examen." Each night I write a prayerful account of my day in five structured steps. Over time, this bedtime ritual has become my tool for slowing down and noticing.

Step One. By writing the words, "Yes, Lord, you are here," I acknowledge God's presence around me and within me. This is important because I tend to forget this fact several times a day. Writing these words brings me back to the truth that God doesn't need me to be aware of God's presence in order for God to be present. This is both a comforting and a humbling truth; comforting because God exists independently of my capacity to pay attention (*and there was much rejoicing!*) and humbling because I so rarely do pay attention. Now, the Tech is not to blame for my lack of awareness, though it would make a neat and tidy scapegoat. Rather, the Tech raises the difficulty setting on my ability to notice from "hard" to "expert" by providing shiny new distractions on a daily basis. But these five simple words—"Yes, Lord, you are here"—ground me in the reality that God moves in and through everything, my distractions included. After writing these words, I listen and I breathe. And something, one huge or tiny thing, detaches from my consciousness, and I write it down. This is the best example of God's presence for the day. When I see it scribbled on the page, I realize that it's not the Lord who is here with me. I realize that I am here with the Lord.

Step Two. After opening myself up to God's presence, I give thanks for all the ways I felt blessed today. They can be as simple as sweater weather or a BLT (where the bacon is nice and lean: I love that). Or they can be as momentous as hearing the ocean's heartbeat in the pounding surf or meeting the woman who would eventually marry me—me of all people. Saving these blessings by putting them down on paper functions as the outward sign of something that happens within. Every blessing is permanent, no matter how quickly it may come and go. Blessings sink down to the bedrock of the soul and stack up around it like the rocky debris that civil engineers use to keep river currents from eroding bridge supports. As the current of today's instantaneous world pulls us along more swiftly every day, pausing to count blessings is as important as ever. Counting blessings is something grandmas tell you to do, and you know what? Grandmas know a thing or two.

Step Three. I reflect on the events of the day and focus on one that brought me closer to or pushed me farther from God. With no time to reflect during the day, I rely on these few minutes at bedtime to watch my day in slow motion. Every action and inaction has the potential either to move me closer to God or to put another brick in the wall that I erect to keep God out. More often than not, the events of my day are fairly mundane, so chances are that I probably didn't notice my relationship with God changing. But it did—for better or worse. Reflecting on both mundane and extraordinary events helps me sort out where exactly I am in my walk with Jesus Christ.

Step Four. I reflect on a particular encounter or conversation with an individual during which I either did or did not fulfill my promises as a disciple of Jesus Christ. These promises derive from Jesus' instructions, and they are fairly uncomplicated: Love God. Love other people. Serve the poor and neglected. Don't let the world snooker you with quick fixes and painless answers. Of course, *uncomplicated* doesn't mean "easy." As I reflect on the day's encounter, I thank God for God's presence in it or ask forgiveness that I didn't realize God was addressing me through the other person. Taking time with this step often reveals uncomfortable truths about my willingness to serve God every day. On the other hand, every once in a while I will meet someone who so radiates the love of God that I can't help but notice and drink it in.

Step Five. I read what I have written and write a sentence about tomorrow in light of what happened today. The first four steps allow me to stop and process my day. Amidst all the distractions and immediacy of life in the Tech-driven world, carving out ten to fifteen precious minutes to reflect is all that stands between me and total system failure, a blue screen of death for my sanity.[†] But

---

[†] *Blue screen of death*: What often happens to computers running the Windows operating system when the system crashes (usually when you're on the last page of your paper and haven't saved in a while). On Macs, this screen is gray and much less prevalent, but still feels like a kick to the teeth when it happens.

this work isn't complete without seeing past the reflection to the future beyond. And so the final step collects the day's blessings and reflections and distills from them a few words of discernment about tomorrow's walk with Christ. I read what I have written (or scrawled, in my case). And again, I listen and breathe. And something else detaches in the form of a prayer to God: "Lord, grant me focus for tomorrow," or "Lord, I need practice welcoming people," or "Lord, help me slow down."

WORDS THAT SHIMMER

The first thing to go when my days reach capacity and then start spilling over into my necessary hours of REM sleep is, more often than not, my study of the Bible. Of course, the moment I decide that I have no time to read Scripture is the precise moment when I need to the most. In these times, a quick glance through the Sermon on the Mount—like I'm browsing a *Rolling Stone* at the newsstand—won't get it done. Rather, I need to combat my presumed busyness and importance by taking time with Scripture, by slowing down enough to notice God encountering me in the words of the Bible. I do this with an old monastic technique called *Lectio Divina* (Divine Reading).

This form of study combines the ingredients of reading, praying, and contemplating in a large mixing bowl of silence. *Lectio Divina* cannot be accomplished quickly and therefore provides a perfect antidote for our instantaneous world. Here's the version of the practice as I received it.

Begin with a short prayer asking God for guidance. (This, by the way, is a good way to start whatever you are doing, whether it's Bible study or grocery shopping.)

Pick a short passage of Scripture, not more than a dozen or so verses. Passages longer than a dozen verses are too long for one sitting. If you are studying a longer story, then break it up into manageable chunks. I find that having a copy of the text with simply the words and nothing else helps my concentration. Copy and paste the verses from an online Bible into your word processor and then remove the chapter and verse numbers along with any editorial headings and notes that might distract you from the words. Because of their narrative nature, the Gospels are often the richest part of the Bible to explore with *Lectio Divina*, but you can study other parts this way as well.

Read your passage aloud slowly with concentration. Did you get that? Read it out loud. Doing this is important for two reasons. First, reading aloud involves your body. You breathe and speak and engage your diaphragm. The more facets of yourself (mental, physical, spiritual, emotional) that you bring to your study of Scripture, the better. Second, reading aloud forces you to make interpretive choices about the tone and character of dialogue that you would not make reading silently. Doing this increases your interaction with the text.

Sit in silence for a minute. I mean this: a full minute. It's longer than you think, like brushing your teeth. The silence acts as an incubator for the words now growing within you. The problem comes when you start checking your cell phone's clock every twenty seconds, hoping the minute is over. This, you might guess, is distracting. The best way to keep track of your silence is to create a minute-long track of silence on iTunes and then make a playlist with the silent minute followed by a soft, soothing song to bring you out of it (in other words, not Queen or glam rock in general, except perhaps the slow bit of "Bohemian Rhapsody").

Read the passage again. Yes, again! Remember, you are taking time with Scripture. No one-and-dones here. This time as you read aloud, notice any words or phrases that shimmer for you. They may jump off the page and smack you in the mouth, or they may draw you toward them so that you realize after a moment that your head is inches from the page.

Sit in silence for another minute. Let the particular word or phrase that shimmered start incubating and growing within.

Meditate on that word or phrase for as long as you need to. Say it in your mind or aloud. Let it hover in the air around you as you sit silently. Let it wrap you up and hold you because, after all, this word is of God and what better way to be wrapped up and held? See what other words come up from the depths of your soul to mingle and combine with the shimmering word. Then pray to God using all of them.

Read the passage aloud a third time. Reinsert your word or phrase into the passage for safekeeping. It will be there the next time you study the text, but next time another word might shimmer instead.

Sit in silence for another minute.

Last, thank God for God's presence in your life and in your study. The whole time is prayer, but a dedicated word of thanks at the end of the time is always a good thing.

Lectio Divina can be done in groups with only a slight variation of the above instructions. Ask different people to read the passage aloud, and have one person be the timekeeper for the silence (or use the iTunes trick). After the second reading, share with one another the words or phrases that shimmer for you, but save commenting on them for later. In place of the meditation step, converse with one another about your words and phrases and anything else that this encounter with Scripture dredges up.

The fruits that come from the slow reading and silence of *Lectio Divina* remind me that faster and louder don't necessarily mean better. Even so, half an hour studying a dozen verses of Scripture often seems like a waste of time. I could read a couple chapters in that period! I could, but in my normal frantic pace, I might miss the word of God that is waiting patiently for me to notice it so that it can plant itself within me and grow.

JESUS IN THE DETAILS

From Creation at the beginning of Genesis to the last words of the prophet Malachi, the first testament of the Bible covers events in broad strokes—and it must, for centuries pass at the turn of a page. Civilizations rise and fall. Kings are crowned and dethroned. While the New Testament covers a much shorter period of time and examines the lives of fewer people, there is still hardly space on the page to paint events in detail. First-person Bible study adds the detail.

In first-person Bible study, which again derives from St. Ignatius (that guy had some really good ideas) and from the practice of ancient Jewish rabbis, you enter the text through the eyes of one of the characters. You see, listen, taste, touch, and smell as that character. Through this method, the text leaps off the page, and you have the opportunity to walk around in the scene and to interact with the other characters. Through this interaction, you fill in the details that the writer had no space to include because the writer was penning a brief account of the gospel of Jesus Christ and not *David Copperfield.*

First-person Bible study offers the benefit of filling in the space between verses of the Bible. When you put yourself in the scene, you strive to expand it and explore it. This expansion is the key that makes first-person study important in a world where sound bites rule the media and Twitter artificially caps the length of thoughts. By painting the detail in between the large brushstrokes of the text, you train yourself to notice the details in your life, the details that the sound bite and the tweet ignore. Jesus encounters us just as much in those details as in the big, newsworthy events of our lives. When we become characters in the text, we practice meeting Jesus in the details.

So, how do you do it? I'm glad you asked. Find a passage of Scripture that attracts or repulses you (oftentimes, passages that repulse are the most fruitful for study). Find a character in the passage. He or she may be a main character such as Peter or Mary or an extra—just a face in the crowd. Your character may be an opponent of Jesus—a Pharisee perhaps or Pontius Pilate. Your character may be Jesus himself. (He's a bit tricky; I've only entered the text as Jesus one time, and it was tough. Better save him until you've had some practice.)

Then write from his or her perspective. If you are in a group, each take a character and act out the scene. Find your motivations.

Improvise more dialogue or extend the scene. First-person study engages the imagination in an expansive effort of delving into the text of the Bible. So dream big. Where did your characters come from right before the scene? What do they do for a living? What kind of family did they grow up in? Every imaginative answer adds flesh and bones and emotion to the characters in the text. But every action, emotion, hope, and fear you give to the character comes from within yourself. Thus this method is a wonderful way to encounter the Scripture honestly and openly.

If you find this practice of engaging Scripture useful and spiritually deepening, try different genres. Write a monologue one time and a letter the next. Write a one-act play, complete with stage directions. Write the inner thoughts behind the outward words. Write a poem or a song. And remember that you are training yourself to notice Jesus in the details of the text and in your life.

A Closing Prayer

Our Tech-driven world is changing rapidly, and we are changing with it. Unlike the great cloud of Christian witnesses that has preceded us, we're not simply earthbound, pavement-pounding disciples of Jesus Christ. Not only are we physical, emotional, and spiritual people: we are now virtual people. Does this fact fundamentally change the faith we have received from our Lord Jesus Christ? No. But the Tech adds a new and pervasive layer to the world that we inhabit, a layer that we digital disciples must train ourselves to peer through as we search for the God who stands under and within all created things. Recall these words from Psalm 139:

> Where could I go to get away from your spirit?
> Where could I go to escape your presence?
> If I went up to heaven, you would be there.
> If I went down to the grave, you would be there too!
> If I could fly on the wings of dawn,
>   stopping to rest only on the far side of the ocean—
> even there your hand would guide me;
> even there your strong hand would hold me tight! (vv. 7-10)

The presence of God fills all of creation, including the worlds that we create in virtual space. These new worlds abound with the certainty of encountering the presence of God in them, even as our real rock, water, and air world still abounds with the movement of God. I offer this prayer for all digital disciples of Jesus Christ to use when we explore these worlds that the Tech makes available to us:

> *Gracious God, your presence abounds in every corner of your creation.*
> *As I wander the paths of the ever-changing and expanding virtual part of that creation, I pray:*
>
> *When I am distracted by the new, the fast, and the shiny,*
> *Give me eyes to see your presence, Lord.*
> *When I allow the Tech to limit my senses,*
> *Give me eyes to see your presence, Lord.*
> *When I fail to remember that you are everywhere,*
> *Give me eyes to see your presence, Lord.*
>
> *When someone reaches out to me,*
> *Help me deepen our connection, Lord.*
> *When I desire my version of other people over the people they actually are,*

Help me deepen our connection, Lord.
When I go no further than fleeting and transient interactions
with other people,
Help me deepen our connection, Lord.

When I allow the virtual world to shrink my life
to the two dimensions of the computer screen,
Help me resist isolation, Lord.
When I ignore the world around me in favor of the virtual one
that I can control,
Help me resist isolation, Lord.

When other people invite me to be a part of their community,
Help me resist isolation, Lord.
When I feel that I have no time at all,
Slow me down, Lord.
When the demands of an immediate world squeeze out every-
thing else,
Slow me down, Lord.
When I fail to give you space to work in my life,
Slow me down, Lord.

Grant me the patience to seek you,
The grace to find you,
And the courage to bring you to all I meet
In both this world and in the virtual ones.
All this I pray in the name of your Son, Jesus Christ,
Who lives and reigns with you and the Holy Spirit,
One God, now and forever. Amen.

GUIDE FOR REFLECTION AND DISCUSSION

1. VIRTUAL PEOPLE

Overview

Simply put, every Internet connection is also an Internet isolation. These dual forces, along with their accompanying opportunities and dangers, generate the reality into which all users step when they employ the Tech. Some of us have never known a world without this reality. Others grew up in a vastly different world, but the Tech has encouraged them and in some cases forced them to adapt. For those of us who are Tech users and followers of Jesus Christ, our current reality has added the virtual dimension to our physical, emotional, and spiritual lives. As digital disciples, we face opportunities and challenges that earlier generations of Christians could never dream up. But this doesn't mean that the wisdom and tradition of our forerunners, along with a good stiff breeze from the Holy Spirit, cannot guide us as we explore this new virtual terrain.

Survey

This survey is designed to help people of various ages locate themselves along the timeline of the Tech's development and demonstrate in microcosm how much the Tech affects their daily lives now. This is an interesting survey to complete in an inter-generational group.

Please check all that apply.

1. When I was in my youth, I listened to
   a) ____ the radio. (*I watched it too; it was encased in a big, curved wooden box.*)
   b) ____ vinyl records. (*If you play it backward, it says that Paul is dead.*)
   c) ____ cassette tapes. (*It was always cued to side B when I wanted to listen to side A.*)
   d) ____ CDs. (*Stick one in the microwave for five seconds. Whoa.*)
   e) ____ downloaded music. (*My iTunes could play for sixteen and a half days before stopping.*)

   My telephone communication consisted of
   a) ____ a party line. (*Mrs. Workman next door always knew the results of our doctor's tests.*)
   b) ____ a rotary phone. (*Shhhhwooooop. Ts-ts-ts-ts-ts. Shhhwooop. Ts-ts. Shhhwoooooooop. Ts-ts-ts-ts-ts-ts.*)
   c) ____ a touchtone phone. (*"To reach a representative, press 4 on your touchtone phone."*)

d) ___ your very own phone line. (*So your mom couldn't nose in on your late-night calls to your bf.*)

e) ___ a cellular phone. (*"Sorry. I dropped you again. I'll call you back when I have better reception."*)

There were this many personal computers in my house:

a) ___ 0 (*Computers were the size of my house.*)

b) ___ 1 (*Mavis Beacon tried to teach me typing. She failed.*)

c) ___ 2 (*Dad had a new one in the study and the rest of the family got to play with Paint on the old one.*)

d) ___ 3 (*Each of us kids had his or her own computer.*)

e) ___ 4+ (*I grew up at NASA's Houston operations center.*)

I played on this video game system:

a) ___ Video games? What video games? (*I had a backyard and an imagination.*)

b) ___ Arcade games (*Those space invaders mesmerized me with their pretty patterns.*)

c) ___ Atari 2600 (*Pong. Enough said.*)

d) ___ Nintendo Entertainment System (*It was the home of the world's most famous Italian plumber.*)

e) ___ Sega Genesis (*No matter what I did, I always managed to crash Sonic on those spikes.*)

f) ___ Playstation (*Three dimensions. I can move around in three dimensions. This is amazing.*)

g) ___ Xbox (*Until you played it, you had no idea why the game was called Halo.*)

h) ___ Wii (*Wii Sports is still the most fun game for the system.*)

(If your system isn't listed, choose the one that was concurrent with yours. For example, if you had a Nintendo 64, choose letter *f*.)

2. I use the Internet
   a) ___ I don't use the Internet.
   b) ___ once a week.
   c) ___ a few times a week.
   d) ___ every day.
   e) ___ every hour.

3. I get my news from
   a) ___ the newspaper.
   b) ___ NPR.
   c) ___ network nightly news.
   d) ___ twenty-four-hour cable news stations (CNN, MSNBC, FoxNews).
   e) ___ John Stewart and Stephen Colbert.
   f) ___ blogs.
   g) ___ news websites.
   h) ___ Facebook.

4. With my cell phone, I primarily
   a) ___ make phone calls. What else is it for?
   b) ___ text. Text. Text.
   c) ___ check my e-mail, get GPS directions, listen to music, play games, tune my guitar, and wash my car. I have an iPhone. (It doesn't actually do that last one.)
   d) ___ use it as a paperweight.

e) ___ wait a sec. What's a cell phone? What? It's not 1997? What year is it?

f) ___ drop it in the toilet accidentally.

5. When I am driving to a place I've never been, I
   a) ___ call ahead and ask for directions.
   b) ___ look at the map in the glove box.
   c) ___ print directions off Google Maps or Mapquest.
   d) ___ plug in my portable GPS and let a pleasant-sounding British voice guide me with turn-by-turn instructions.

6. Facebook friends:
   I have this many Facebook friends. ___
   I have this many Facebook friends with whom I actually care about keeping in contact. ___
   I do not have a Facebook account. ___

7. Personal computers:
   My first personal computer was portable. ___ Yes ___ No
   My current personal computer is portable. ___ Yes ___ No
   I have never owned a personal computer. ___

8. I know what these acronyms stand for:

(1)	(2)	(3)
___ HTTP	___ LOL	___ LFG
___ TCP/IP	___ TTFN	___ AFK
___ HTML	___ BRB	___ DPS
___ CSS	___ JK (or j/k)	___ DoT
___ URL	___ IDK	___ PUG

Knowing a majority in column 1 means you have some knowledge of how the Internet works or of Web design or you just like acronyms. Knowing a majority in column 2 means you understand the language of the nearly extinct AOL Instant Messenger, which has migrated to SMS text messaging. Knowing a majority in col-umn 3 means you play or have played World of Warcraft *(or another MMORPG).* †

Questions

1. I mentioned that removing the Internet would be like removing a body's central nervous system. What do you think would happen in society if the Internet were to disappear? What would be the positive and negative effects of its disappearance?

2. In what ways do you engage in trans-social behavior? How has the level of your engagement changed over the last five years? ten years? twenty years?

3. In what ways do you monitor the information you publish about yourself on the Internet? Are your birthday, phone number, and street address available? Are pictures of your children online?

4. When going on vacation, do you mention it online? If you have not thought through these and similar questions, sit down with your family and discuss Tech-based privacy issues.

---

† HyperText Transfer Protocol; Transmission Control Protocol/Internet Protocol; HyperText Markup Language; Cascading Style Sheets; Uniform Resource Locator; Laughing Out Loud; Ta Ta for Now; Be Right Back; Just Kidding; I Don't Know; Looking for Group; Away from Keyboard; Damage per Second; Damage over Time; Pickup Group.

5. In what ways do you see yourself in the description of Internet addiction (found in the section "In-Game Experience")? If you fully identify with the description, what have you done to address this very difficult challenge?

6. In the passage from 1 Thessalonians, how do you think Paul's message to the world of the first century translates to our Tech-driven modern world?

7. Before moving on to the rest of the book, register your first reactions to the questions posed at the end of the first section of this chapter:

   • How do the Tech's simultaneous forces of connection and isolation affect our walks with Christ?
   • How does living in a virtual world influence living in both the physical and the spiritual ones?
   • How do we maintain the body of Christ when the physical bodies we see and touch in church expand to include the virtual bodies we encounter online?
   • What place does prayer have in our instantaneous Tech-driven world?
   • Where do we keep our knowledge of God when our preferred method of storing information has shifted to the external?
   • How do we resist isolation while remaining plugged into the Series of Tubes?
   • How do we continue in the tradition of the personal nature of the ministry of Jesus in lives that are increasingly siphoned off into remote, disembodied, virtual space?

2. FROM CONNECTION TO COMMUNION

Overview

Following Christ through the terrain of the virtual world involves being aware of the presence of God encoded into the infrastructure of all things—both physical and virtual. This presence is the fertile soil in which God plants the seeds of the religious life: namely, the impulse to gather. We make connections online every day, and each one of these connections holds the potential to blossom into something deeper—the communion that is the natural outgrowth of recognizing and celebrating God's weaving movement in our lives. This weaving movement stitches together the new ad hoc house churches, which meet online whenever people discover and discuss God's presence. The Internet offers such great opportunity for connection because the limiting nature of *place* has no ability to keep people from finding one another. The difficult task comes when we desire connection to deepen into communion.

Questions

1. When was the last time you thanked God for creating someone else? What were the circumstances surrounding that gratitude? What is your relationship with the other person?

2. C. S. Lewis envisions human life "rather like a very complicated tree." What does your part of this tree look like? To whom are you connected? Who makes up your roots and canopy? Draw your tree and then reflect on how you first came in contact with your connections. How did the Tech play a part in this contact? How does it now?

3. How often do you pause to thank God for God's presence in your gatherings, both in real life and online? What prevents you from this kind of pausing and reflection?

4. Have you ever participated in an online house church as described in the chapter? What was your experience? How did you follow up this experience to deepen connection into communion? How have you translated online house church experience into real-world action?

5. What things are right in front of you all the time that you never see? How does the Tech's constant stimulation of the senses affect your ability to appreciate the permanent things in your life?

6. Where do you see God in your virtual connections? What has happened in your life that you once labeled as "coincidence," but you've since relabeled as "God's connecting presence"?

3. REMOTE INTIMACY

Overview

Connection and isolation are inseparable, especially in the virtual world of the Tech. How well we followers of Christ orient ourselves away from the danger of isolation marks us as successful or unsuccessful digital disciples. A wall of separation grows up around anyone who uses the Tech. The wall separates the user from the people physically close by and from the people on the other end of virtual connections. This wall is a natural and unavoidable part of using the Tech. For those of us who have grown up using the Tech and for those who use it all the time, communication from behind the wall can feel more natural and more comfortable than face-to-face communication. We run the risk of developing the fantasy of remote intimacy with people whom we know only through the Tech. The remoteness of the Tech can lead to a seemingly no-consequence environment like the one in which cyberbullying flourishes. But God is in the business of removing isolation and repairing relationships. We can participate in knocking down the wall.

Questions

1. The Tech isolates each of us, but because that isolation comes in so many shapes and sizes, our particular flavors of isolation differ as well. How does the Tech isolate you specifically? What happened to allow you to notice this isolation? What steps are you taking to address it?

2. Where do you see yourself in the description of the three couch dwellers? How has the remoteness of trans-social communication affected your interaction with others?

3. Jesus was and is a wall breaker. What walls that you put up are you unwilling to let Jesus break down? How do your personal walls and the wall of the Tech interact?

4. Christianity is a difficult religion to practice alone. Review your walk with Jesus Christ. How has it differed when you have been with other people as opposed to alone?

5. How has remote intimacy affected your life? How did the avatar you created for someone else differ from the real, living, breathing person? How did that person's avatar differ from you?

6. How has cyberbullying impacted your life? Have you been bullied? Have you done the bullying? Has a child or friend been a victim or an attacker? Describe how the Tech and the wall of separation played a role in your experience of bullying.

7. In the parable from Luke, the father repairs his relationships with the sons who have isolated themselves. How can you invite God into your life to accomplish this same type of repair?

4. EMPTY MINDS AND DISPOSABLE BODIES

Overview

The Tech not only isolates us from others; it also isolates us from ourselves. Because of its external nature, the Tech naturally devalues the mind and body, thus projecting an illusion that the former is superfluous and the latter disposable. Followers of Jesus Christ know that the Word became flesh in order to help us find within ourselves the image and likeness of God, which is God's original gift to us. But when the Tech isolates the functions usually ascribed to our minds and bodies and then programs those functions into external sources, accessing the image and likeness of God within becomes very challenging indeed. We outsource our minds when we use the Tech to do simple things that humans have been doing "in house" (that is, in the mind) for thousands of years. We prize information over knowledge, so "knowing" Jesus Christ has become more difficult. The senses we use to seek God's presence in our lives are reduced by 60 percent when we use the Tech; therefore, we must strive even harder to be attentive. Living sacramentally means using our senses and our minds both to seek God and to bring God to other people. This sacramental living takes Jesus' incarnation out of its historical context and brings it into the present through the media of our lives.

Questions

1. What is your experience with the version of "death" found in video games? What are your associations between the thousand different ways to die (and, for that matter, to kill) in video games and the real, physical permanence of death?

2. How have you evolved (or devolved) from *Homo sapiens* to *Homo interwebs*? How has the Tech made you better or smarter? What small tasks could you once do in your mind that you now find either difficult or inconvenient to do without a machine of one sort or another?

3. How has outsourcing your mind affected your life as a follower of Jesus Christ? Think especially about the following areas: Bible study, worship, prayer, and engagement with theological principles.

4. Information deepening into knowledge is one step in the process of knowing Jesus Christ. The next step is for knowledge to deepen into wisdom. How has the Tech impacted your

ability to develop wisdom, as elders of bygone years would have understood the concept?

5. How do we make up for the loss of our bodies in the virtual world? How do we trend toward the fullness that Jesus offers us when we use the Tech, which necessarily diminishes our capacity to live as incarnate beings?

6. Considering the example about the ocean, how do you personally rehabilitate the senses that you fail to use when engaging the Tech?

7. What sacramental actions do you take part in that help you connect to God and other people?

8. What place does the Incarnation have in your life? Is it a historical event or a present reality or some combination of the two? (Or something else altogether?) How has the Tech changed your conception of Incarnation?

5. GOOGLING PRAYER

Overview

The Tech has made our world instantaneous. Our daily walk with Jesus, however, happens not in minutes, but in moments—glorious indefinite moments filled with God's presence. In these moments we can practice responding to that presence, which is one definition of *prayer*. Rather than ask God to respond to us (the model that the Tech has encoded into us), our prayer is best directed at making ourselves open to God's initiating creativity in our lives. This is a slow process that does not work on the kind of time on which the Tech runs; rather, it works on a special kind of time measured by events and yearnings and not by minutes and hours. Whenever we feel hurried and harried by the Tech and our instantaneous world, a glorious indefinite moment with God is always waiting to happen within this special kind of time.

Questions

1. Navigate to www.beloit.edu/mindset/ and find the list for your graduation year. Compare it with the current list. If you attended college prior to the beginning of the list, try compiling a list for your graduation year and see how vastly it differs from today's.

2. Google *prayer* the day you read this. You'll find that the total numbers of hits will be well more than the seventy-six million received in August 2010. Ponder the implications of an Internet that expands so rapidly that there are so many million more hits on the word *prayer* today than when that earlier search took place.

3. What does *prayer* mean to you? What has it meant at various stages of your life? How do you connect with the definition that prayer is responding to God rather than asking God to respond to us?

4. Aslan tells Jill Pole: "You would not have called to me unless I had been calling to you." What is God calling to you about? How will you respond? How will the Tech hinder or advance that call?

5. What is your breath prayer? How often does it bubble to the surface? Is it a thought, a feeling, a verbal utterance, or something else entirely?

6. Are you too busy, not busy enough, or just the right amount of busy? Does the Tech make your life more composed or more chaotic? In either case, how so?

7. When do you fit following Jesus Christ into your busy life? Do you make time for your life as a disciple before you schedule everything else, or after?

6. TECH SABBATH

Overview

We spend much of our lives in the instantaneous, disembodied, remotely intimate, trans-social world of the Tech. This is not evil or inherently harmful. But when we reach a point that we never slow down or interact with our physical bodies or connect face-to-face, we are no longer living the life that makes following Jesus Christ the primary priority. The practices in this chapter have helped anchor Christians within the constant that is God so that we are not swept away by the modern current of impermanence. By practicing a Tech Sabbath, we can slow down in the midst of the instantaneous world and notice God's presence in our lives. We can use St. Ignatius's "Examen," a five-step process of reflective prayer. We can engage in *Lectio Divina*, the slow, prayerful, contemplative reading of Scripture that happens within a cone of silence. We can enter the text of the Bible through first-person Bible study, in which we become a character in the text and explore all the details that aren't mentioned on the page. These practices help us notice Jesus in the details of our lives.

Questions

1. Do you remember a time when you could have consulted the Tech but consciously decided not to? If so, describe your experience. If not, try it!

2. Take a single day's Tech Sabbath. What was your experience? How difficult did you find not using the Tech? How did you feel during the day? How did you feel afterward?

3. During your Tech Sabbath, what was the piece of the Tech you found most difficult to give up? What was the easiest? Why? How could you divest yourself of some of the Tech on a more permanent basis?

4. Try the five-step "Examen" at the end of a day. Which step did you find most difficult? Which step did you find easiest? Why? What about your relationship with God did you

uncover? What detached from your consciousness that you may need to address in the future?

5. Try *Lectio Divina*. Which passage did you pick and why? What was your experience during the minutes of silence? What pattern emerged in the "words that shimmer" for you? What did you discern God saying to you from within the text?

6. Enter into Scripture from a first-person perspective. Who did you decide to be and why? What did your engagement with the text tell you about your life?

7. Choose at least one of these practices and experiment with it for at least a month. Is there one that may become a permanent practice for you?

8. Finally, write a personal prayer to God detailing your experience with the Tech. Ask God to open you up to all the possibilities that God gives to you. And thank God for being present in all facets of your life.

ACKNOWLEDGMENTS

Many people helped and guided me along the path that eventually wandered past the creation of the book that you hold in your hands. This space has room for only a handful of their names, but I give thanks to God for each of you all the same.

Special thanks to my editor, Ron, who took this n00b of a writer, polished him up, dusted off his jacket, and made him presentable to the world. Thanks also to the whole staff at Abingdon Press, especially Julie and Desiree, and, of course, to Audrey, who God blessed (cursed?) to have the same sense of humor as I do, or else this book might never have been. The people at Abingdon are gracious and lovely, and I haven't met one yet with whom I wouldn't want to share a pew on Sunday.

Thanks to all the folks through whom the mysterious machinations of the Internet brought me to the attention of Abingdon. To Sonua, who didn't have to e-mail Audrey. To Liz, who didn't have to repost the video that Sonua saw. To Google, who didn't have to invent Google alerts, which brought Sonua to Liz. To Joss Whedon, who didn't have to be awesome enough to have a vociferous and loyal fanbase, of which Sonua, Liz, and I are members. And to Stephen Colbert, who didn't have to invent the truly hilarious and informative show on which I based my video Bible studies, one of which includes a reference to Whedon's *Buffy the Vampire Slayer*.

Thanks to Kathy and Brian, who read more than one version of my seminary thesis, which turned out to be the 156 pages I needed to write in preparation for writing this book. Thanks also for encouraging me to start blogging after seminary.

Thanks to the members of Spectrum Blade and the Scholomance Debate Team, my two guilds in *World of Warcraft*. Please know that the friendships I made with you over the Internet between 2006 and 2008 were quite meaningful to me, even though I tend to excoriate WoW in these pages.

Thanks to the congregation and staff of St. Stephen's, who had to put up with me immediately after I used my vacation time to write this book.

And of course, thanks to my family for their support during the writing of this book and for reading my blog since the beginning. Your encouragement and love mean the world to me.

Finally, to Leah, who is God's greatest blessing in my life. We are getting married twenty-three days from the writing of these acknowledgments, and I can't wait to spend the rest of a "long and silly" life with you.

ABOUT THE AUTHOR

The Reverend Adam Thomas was ordained to the Episcopal priesthood in 2008 at the age of twenty-five, making him one of the first priests from the Millennial generation. His unique voice in the faith community emanates from a combination of his youth, honesty, humor, and tech-savvy nature. A self-described nerd, Adam writes the blog wherethewind.com, belongs to the Christian Century Blogging Community and Day1.org, and knows everything about *Buffy the Vampire Slayer*.